Hockey Plays and Strategies

Ryan Walter

Mike Johnston

Human Kinetics

Library of Congress Cataloging-in-Publication Data

Walter, Ryan, 1958-
Hockey plays and strategies / Ryan Walter and Mike Johnston.
    p. cm.
Includes index.
ISBN-13: 978-0-7360-7634-0 (soft cover)
ISBN-10: 0-7360-7634-4 (soft cover)
 1. Hockey--Offense. 2. Hockey--Coaching. I. Johnston, W. Michael II. Title.
GV848.7.W35 2010
796.962'2--dc22

2009026623

ISBN-10: 0-7360-7634-4 (print)
ISBN-13: 978-0-7360-7634-0 (print)

Acquisitions Editor: Justin Klug; **Developmental Editor:** Kevin Matz; **Assistant Editor:** Scott Hawkins; **Copyeditor:** Patricia MacDonald; **Indexer:** Dan Connolly; **Graphic Designer:** Kim McFarland; **Graphic Artist:** Kim McFarland; **Cover Designer:** Keith Blomberg; **Photographer (cover):** Jim McIsaac/Getty Images Sport; **Art Manager:** Kelly Hendren; **Associate Art Manager:** Alan L. Wilborn; **Illustrator:** Lineworks, Inc. and Alan L. Wilborn; **Printer:** Versa Press

Human Kinetics books are available at special discounts for bulk purchase. Special editions or book excerpts can also be created to specification. For details, contact the Special Sales Manager at Human Kinetics.

Printed in the United States of America   10 9 8 7 6 5 4 3 2 1

The paper in this book is certified under a sustainable forestry program.

Human Kinetics
Web site: www.HumanKinetics.com

United States: Human Kinetics
P.O. Box 5076
Champaign, IL 61825-5076
800-747-4457
e-mail: humank@hkusa.com

Canada: Human Kinetics
475 Devonshire Road Unit 100
Windsor, ON N8Y 2L5
800-465-7301 (in Canada only)
e-mail: info@hkcanada.com

Europe: Human Kinetics
107 Bradford Road
Stanningley
Leeds LS28 6AT, United Kingdom
+44 (0) 113 255 5665
e-mail: hk@hkeurope.com

Australia: Human Kinetics
57A Price Avenue
Lower Mitcham, South Australia 5062
08 8372 0999
e-mail: info@hkaustralia.com

New Zealand: Human Kinetics
P.O. Box 80
Torrens Park, South Australia 5062
0800 222 062
e-mail: info@hknewzealand.com

E4627

Hockey Plays
and Strategies

Contents

Foreword

Ryan Walter and Mike Johnston are great coaches who have been around long enough to really understand the game of hockey. Their book, *Hockey Plays and Strategies*, is a great reference for any coach, player, or fan.

Hockey requires a strong blend of physical and mental skills. Players need a solid base of fundamentals—skating, shooting, and passing—before beginning to understand how to play the game. But it's the tactical team skills that are necessary for competing and winning at a high level. And this book will help develop those tactical skills.

In Detroit, we talk about a three-step process for success. The first two steps are work ethic and structure. Work ethic is self-explanatory. Structure, a focus of *Hockey Plays and Strategies*, protects each player. Everyone has a complete understanding of his responsibilities on the ice, which in turn makes everyone quicker. Players can be quick when they know that each teammate will do his part. This leads to an up-tempo game and therefore success.

The third step in the process is skill. Without the work ethic and a solid structure, players such as Lidstrom, Datsyuk, and Zetterberg would still be extremely skilled, but they wouldn't have the continual success they've enjoyed in their careers. In 2008, the Detroit Red Wings won the Stanley Cup. One of the biggest plays in game 4 was a five-on-three penalty kill when Henrik Zetterberg blocked out Sidney Crosby's stick to prevent a goal. That play was a huge reason we went up 3-1 in the series instead of being tied 2-2, and it probably assured Zetterberg the Conn Smythe trophy as playoff MVP and assured us the Stanley Cup. That is an example of a great skill play, but it was also based on good structure.

This book offers advice for both coaches and players. Coaches will learn the strategies necessary for success, and players will find advice to help them understand the demands of the game and their roles within the specific systems and strategies that coaches ask them to perform on the ice. *Hockey Plays and Strategies* is divided into three parts dealing with offensive play, defensive play, and special situations such as power plays, penalty kills, and face-offs. Mike and Ryan's structure of the chapters is easy to follow—they work from the net out and from the opposition's net back, just as a play progresses on the ice. Coaches and players alike will find guidance on the movements and tactics in the most effective offensive and defensive systems in the game. This book also compares the systems and strategies—based on execution, personnel requirements, and their unique advantages and disadvantages—so that coaches can make the best use of a team's talents and prepare for specific opponents, situations, or player combinations.

Most coaches agree that their main responsibility is to help players become the best they can be. Understanding hockey's complicated plays and strategies is a key factor in creating successful players. A coach should always look for ways to provide the information necessary to help a group of athletes come together and succeed as a team. This book goes a long way in providing that information.

Mike Babcock

Preface

In previous work as authors, Ryan and I focused on the leadership angle and the so-called intangibles in the sport of hockey. When approached about writing a book that involved breaking the game down into all its technical components and strategies, we were both very excited about the opportunity. The game of hockey is presently played in almost every country, with millions of participants worldwide. Although several countries claim ownership of the game, there has been significant sharing of ideas, philosophies, and strategies over the years. All countries have adapted their approach to include what they believe are the key ingredients to put them in a position to claim world titles. This book includes several strategies and tactics prevalent in the games of successful European countries while focusing on ones we have used with teams or observed being used with teams we have coached against. Understanding the tactics and strategy involved in the game is critical for on-ice success.

Hockey Plays and Strategies is broken down into three primary sections dealing with offensive play, defensive play, and special situations. Does great defensive play win championships, as the saying goes? Not necessarily—if you look at the results of the major professional leagues in baseball, football, basketball, and hockey, there have been an equal number of dynasties whose teams are remembered for their offensive prowess. It is our belief that a good balance is best, and then as a coach your natural tendency will be to lean slightly toward the offensive or defensive side depending on your style and comfort level. The final section in the book discusses the strategies and tactics involved in face-offs and also discusses in detail how coaches can separate themselves from the pack with their bench-management skills. One of the greatest coaches in the game, Scotty Bowman, was always known as a master when it came to bench-management skills.

The sequence for the offensive and defensive chapters works from the net out and from the opposition's net back. Offensive chapters cover the breakout, neutral zone attack and regroups, offensive zone entry (including odd-man rushes), the attack zone, and power plays. Defensive chapters cover the forecheck, neutral zone forecheck and backcheck, defensive zone entry (including odd-man defensive play), defensive zone coverage, and penalty kill.

We have attempted to explain in detail where applicable the key teaching points involved in executing the systems discussed. As mentioned in the book, it is not the system you choose that will make you successful; it is how effectively the players execute the system and whether you as a coach can get the players to execute consistently every game. When there are breakdowns, you need to know where to look to make corrections. Understanding the key teaching points will help in this area as well as allow the players to grasp the concepts easier. Our goal in writing this book is to give both coaches and players the information they need in order to succeed. Enjoy!

Introduction: Preamble on Coaching

Coaching is a very complex job. We have found through experience and also in our previous book *Simply the Best – Insights and Strategies from Great Coaches* that there is an "art and science" side to coaching. The "art" refers to instincts and feel while the "science" refers to technical and physiological. This book primarily deals with the technical side of the game, with only Chapter 12 (Bench Management and Line Changes) focusing on the art of coaching. Therefore we would be remiss if we didn't highlight a few more key details on the art of coaching which are directly linked to the systems and strategies in the book. Developing your team identity, understanding teaching and learning and conducting good practices all fit into being a well rounded coach.

All great organizations and great teams have a clear identity. Teams are recognized as being hard working, dynamic offensively, gritty and tough, fast, young, or sound defensively. You know what the identity of a team is simply by observing how they operate. The saying that a team is a reflection of their coach is so true. It is the coach and management that impart an identity on the team by the players they select, the system they play, how they practice, and generally how they behave on and off the ice. Unfortunately many coaches miss this step in preparing for the season and as a result they are not really anything. They look different from game to game, there is no base of "who they are" to fall back on in tough times and the coach will constantly be reacting to situations with quick fix solutions but never really getting anywhere. Remember, if your team doesn't know your identity, you are in trouble. A team is much like a corporation or business – those with a clear identity and purpose which everyone buys into, flourish, and those without one, sink. Therefore this is one of the most important things you can do in preparing for a successful season. Is it difficult? No. Basically there are three steps in identifying what type of team you want to be.

1. Picture yourself watching your team in late January; see them on the ice for practice, in game action, training off the ice, at a restaurant for a team meal, and possibly even in the classroom.

2. Now write down everything you want to be observing five months from now. What personal and physical qualities do you want to see? How does the team act/behave? How do they train? How do they treat each other? How do they handle pressure? How does your team play? We all want a big, fast, skilled, and sound defensive team, but we all know it is not realistic to have everything. What is most important to

you? Discuss this with your staff. What values do you want to impart to your team?

3. Once you have thoroughly developed your identity with your staff, it is important to now inform the team of your identity as well as other parties who are close to your team (e.g., parents, manager, support staff, and media). Constantly reinforce the identity throughout the season by repeating it over and over again. This is how we practice, this is how we play, this is how we act. Your players will get it over time and eventually take on this identity and more importantly take ownership for it. Challenge your staff and team to come up with a slogan, logo, or song that exemplifies your identity.

Teaching and Learning

As a coach, you may find yourself asking, *Why aren't they learning?* or *Why does he always do that? Doesn't he get it?* The first place to look for answers is your coaching strategy, because if there is no learning, there is no coaching taking place. This book is all about teaching. Sometimes you will get frustrated with your players' progress, but you need to recognize that coaching has many challenges. Don't get caught in the cycle of looking at reasons why you can't win. Instead, challenge yourself and your staff to find a way.

No matter what level you are coaching, it is important to never assume. If you believe that players should know certain things because of their age, you may be eager to start at a higher level. However, you should always start with the basics. When using this book, chose a system or strategy and then review the key teaching points. Teach it to your team by using basic drills and then progressing to more complicated or involved drills. Be careful to resist the urge to change when it is not going well. Progress at a pace appropriate for the team and age level. I suggest you use a checklist so that you can monitor the progression of the team and of specific positions. A check list involves all aspects of your team play written down one side of the page and then as you practice each you make note of the date beside it. This will keep your coaching staff focused on what has to be done, what needs to be done and eliminate moving too fast. You can even note what date you would like to have taught that particular system or strategy to the team. For instance with the power play, early in the year the priority will be on breaking out and zone set up for a five-on-four. As the year moves along and team competency progresses you will start to focus more on the five-on-three and four-on-three power play options. Accept that with only so much practice time you can't do everything at once—so develop priorities.

It is often the basic skills or teaching points within a system that separate the top players and teams. Most players are motivated and willing to learn or develop in any area that will help elevate their play or create longevity in their careers. Show them a plan to be successful, work on developing it, and stay strong when your plan is challenged. It is not the particular system that wins championships; it is all about quality of execution.

Practices

Although many players would much rather play the games, it is important to remember that you develop through practice. Statistically, the average player in a game takes one or two shots on goal, makes 15 to 20 passes, and is on the ice for 20 out of the 60 minutes. According to one of the more revealing statistics from the 2002 Olympic Games in Salt Lake City, elite players had the puck on their sticks for less than 90 seconds for the whole game. Most players were under a minute. During a well-run practice, a player should be able to take 30-plus shots, make 50 passes, receive the puck 50 times, and have the puck on his stick at least 25 percent of the time. Therefore it takes approximately 15 games to simulate the amount of skill repetition that takes place in an effectively run 60-minute practice.

Listed below are eight keys to maximize your practice time. Ice sessions are expensive and difficult to obtain, so it is important to get the most out of each.

1. **Prepare yourself and your coaching staff.**
   - Use a set practice form which has room to explain the execution of the drill, teaching points and length of time. Keep your practice forms in a book, or file them away.
   - All coaches on the ice should know the drill sequence and teaching points. The head coach should outline who is responsible for teaching the drill to the team and where the coaches will be positioned once the drill begins.
   - Come to the rink with energy and energize your staff. Players will feed off you, and these sessions are what they look forward to all week.

2. **Provide practice rules.**
   - To properly manage the ice, especially when the acoustics in most rinks are not good, it is critical to have set practice rules. Inform the team that for everyone to benefit, the rules need to be adhered to. One rule that can often speed up practice is "every time the whistle blows all players come in quickly to the coach and then after the next drill is described go to your specific area and get ready to go" Depending on how much help the head coach has try to get the players to collect the pucks and set them up in the appropriate area.

3. **Create a positive learning environment.**
   - Use positive talk and positive gestures.
   - Talk to every player every practice. Even if it is about the movie they saw last night, your staff should never leave the arena without having touched base with every player.
   - Provide feedback throughout practice. Try to do it constructively, and do not stop the drill. Get to the players while they are waiting in line. Bring the group together only for key points or messages.

4. **Balance individual skill with small-group and team-play work.**
   - Vary the drill formations and alignments to work on team play and individual skills.

○ Use stations for small-group skill work. This is effective for concentrated effort and high repetition.

5. **Repeat, repeat, and repeat again.**

   ○ Players develop through the "agony of repetition"—those are the facts.

   ○ Keep the players moving throughout practice; activity is key. This will develop endurance and ensure that they're making the best use of practice time by always working on skills.

   ○ Have a set bank of practice drills to teach your system's plays.

   ○ Repeat drills often, but change the focus or teaching points.

   ○ Constantly push the team for better execution.

6. **Incorporate challenges and fun games.**

   ○ Open and close practice with a bang.

   ○ Challenge yourself to come up with drills that are fun but that also work on key skills.

   ○ Incorporate competitive challenges. Keep score during drills.

7. **Have teaching aids available.**

   ○ Use ropes, tires, balls, spray paint, chairs, and pylons to add to the practice environment.

   ○ Make sure a rink board is also available so that players can visualize what you're explaining. Practice drawing the drills clearly.

8. **Conduct your warm-up and conditioning off the ice.**

   ○ Ice time is valuable, so as much as possible, stretch and warm up off the ice as a group.

   ○ Try to get a conditioning effect by the way you keep the practice moving and by the demands you make on effort throughout practice. Stopping practice and forcing the players to do a conditioning skate is necessary at times, but it is much better to work on conditioning and skill at the same time.

The key to developing players is to catch them doing something right, and the practice environment provides many opportunities for this. Strive to achieve practice perfection and good habits. Coach the players to "think the game"; they will enjoy the game more and get much more out of it.

Key to Diagrams

C	Center
F	Forward
D	Defensive player
LD	Left defensive player
RD	Right defensive player
O	Offensive player
RW	Right Wing
LW	Left Wing
G	Goalie
EX	Extra forward
⟶	Player skating without the puck
∿∿∿⟶	Player skating with the puck
------⟶	Pass
⟹	Shot
⊢	Screen, pick, or block
∿∿∿	Skating backward
‖‖‖	Lateral movement crossover steps

Part I

Offensive Play for Forwards and Defensemen

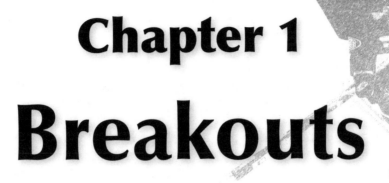

Chapter 1

Breakouts

A breakout is initiated when the puck is in a team's defensive zone. All five skaters and even the goaltender need to be involved to exit the zone successfully. Players react to the position of the puck to initiate or support the breakout. Breakouts can take place in four situations: (1) after a dump-in by the other team; (2) on a rebound off a shot; (3) after an intercepted pass; or (4) when a player takes the puck away from the opposition. The most difficult part in executing a successful breakout is handling pressure from the opposition and completing a good first pass. The first step is to realize where the pressure is coming from so you can execute the appropriate option to escape your defensive zone.

Reading Pressure and Options

When a defenseman picks up the puck to initiate a breakout, he could be faced with three different situations. In the first, there is no forechecking pressure; in the second, the forechecker is 6 feet (1.8 m) or more away; and in the third, the forechecker is right on the defenseman's back.

In most situations the defenseman has mere seconds to make a play, so it is often important to "buy time." To do this effectively you have to fake one way by looking at that option with your eyes while putting the puck in a passing position. The forechecker will often bite on this fake pass, or look-away, and turn his feet in that direction, which will give the defenseman more time to make a play. The art of deception is a skill that must be practiced; once mastered, it provides defensemen with both extra time in a critical area and less chance of being hit.

The following three examples for defensemen all deal with varying forechecking pressure that happens after a dump-in by the other team; after a rebound off a shot; after an intercepted pass; or when a player takes the puck away from the opposition.

1. **No forechecking pressure.** In this situation the defenseman is concerned about getting back quickly, collecting the puck and turning up ice. Check your shoulder as you go back for the puck to read your options. Goaltenders should communicate options to the defenseman retrieving the puck. Simply using a verbal cue such as "time" is enough to let the player know he has an opportunity to look up and turn the puck up ice without having to protect it from pressure. Specific communication calls are critical to successful breakouts because the player retrieving the puck is focused on getting the puck and has limited opportunity to read the other team. His teammates, while moving to support the breakout, have a chance to read the opponent's forechecking pressure. When turning the puck up ice, get your feet moving right away while at the same time keeping the puck at your side in a position to pass. If there are no options, then put the puck out in front of you and jump up ice.

2. **Close forechecking pressure.** When the forechecker is 6 feet (1.8 m) or more away, the defenseman should go back for the puck under control while checking both shoulders to read the forecheck and also the passing options available. This is an important routine to do regardless of the checking pressure. As you get close to the puck, square your feet, glide, and then fake one way and go the other. This will shake the forechecker and give you time to escape or make a quick play. The fake doesn't have to be complicated, just a slight movement one way with your stick or shoulder while tight turning to the other side. Take three quick strides in order to separate from the forechecker, and then make a pass or continue skating.

3. **Quick, hard forechecking pressure.** In this situation the forechecker is right on the defenseman, and it looks as if the defenseman will get hit. When going back for the puck, check both shoulders and then slow down as you approach the puck. Your first priority is to protect the puck while at the same time leaning back against the forechecker to gain control over that player. Absorb his momentum, and either spin away with the puck or rebound off the boards in a position to make a play. Never expose the puck; stay on the defensive side and protect it until you can make a play.

Reacting to Support the Breakout

All three forwards have key positional responsibilities on the breakout. Breakouts are initiated by the defense, and most of the time the primary role of the forwards is to provide support options. The option of having forwards leave the zone early may be a team philosophy or a coaching philosophy, but it is worth considering allowing your wingers to leave the zone early on certain breakout plays—especially since the red line was removed from the game at all levels. The key read for wingers is puck possession and checking pressure; once you see your defenseman or center get the puck under control with minimal forechecking pressure, then move out into the neutral zone and look for the stretch pass (figure 1.1). The pass does not have to be a direct pass; it could be an indirect pass off the boards where the winger can skate into it. This type of strategy is intimidating for the opposition because they will generally move at least one of their Ds back and often they get caught with a soft or loose gap in the neutral zone. They will definitely be worried about giving up a breakaway and as a result may not hold the blue line as tightly. The space between the attacking players and defensive players is generally referred to as the gap. On offense, a loose gap gives you a chance to make plays in front of the defensive team and have more time. The defensive team wants to have a tight gap to eliminate time and space.

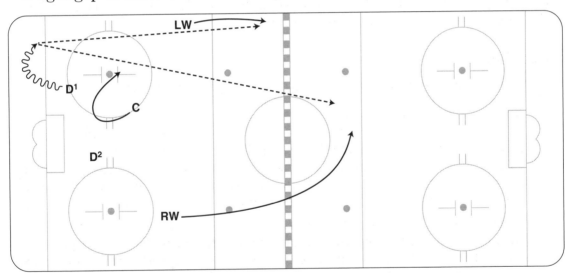

Figure 1.1   Leaving the zone early on the breakout.

Center

The center usually plays low in the defensive zone, but as noted under the section on defensive zone coverage, any forward could be the low player. The player who plays low defensively is usually very good in coverage and breakout situations. Often the low forward is involved in getting the puck back from the opposition, so other than a dumped-in puck, his position on the breakout will seldom vary. The low forward provides the defense with a mid-ice option on all breakouts. If the puck is passed up the boards, then he is in a support position for the winger, who may bring the puck inside, make a direct pass, or chip it off the boards. The center or low forward must be available for a pass but also in a position to react defensively if there is a turnover.

When passes are made up the boards, centers need to come from underneath the pass and skate into a support position. It is important to be cautious in this position because anything could happen, and if a turnover occurs during the breakout, the center or low forward must be ready to defend.

Strong-Side Winger

The strong-side winger on the breakout must be available on the boards for a direct or rimmed puck. We like the winger to be in a higher position above the circles so that the pass from the defenseman or center advances the puck as far up ice as possible. If the other team pinches or closes down on the winger as the pass is being made, then it is important for the winger to fight the battle up higher on the boards. He can try to box out the pinching defenseman by backing into him as the puck is being passed up.. If the winger starts the breakout lower on the boards and not up higher as suggested, then it will take more time and potentially more passes to get over the blue line, which often results in turnovers. The winger must be strong in all board battles because a turnover here may be costly and lead to extended time in the defensive zone and often an opportunity for the opposition to create scoring chances.

Back-Side Winger

The back-side winger on the breakout may skate one of three routes:

1. As the puck advances up the far side, the winger may move across for support and a pass or move to a puck that is chipped off the boards into the neutral zone. The winger coming across creates more options than the winger staying wide, and the success of this strategy relies on short passes or chip plays. Short passes or chip plays are definitely easier to execute than long cross-ice passes, which are often intercepted.

2. As the puck advances up the far side, the winger may stay wide so that they avoid checking pressure from the other team. This wide pass is more difficult to make but once made usually provides more skating room for the winger because he will be on the outside shoulder of the opponent's defense and can drive in the wide lane.

3. Because of the elimination of the red line a few years ago, some coaches like to give the green light for the wide winger to leave the zone early and be available by moving in the neutral zone. This is effective because the opposition will have to back one of their defensemen out of the zone, and as a result the back-side winger can move into open ice much easier as the pass is made. The only problem with doing this is that playing four on four in your defensive zone is more difficult than five on five.

Goaltender

In most leagues goaltenders are restricted in the area they are allowed to handle the puck. At the NHL level, goaltenders may handle the puck anywhere above the goal line and in the trapezoid area below the goal line. Regardless of the level and restrictions, it is important that goaltenders learn to pass the puck up on line changes (figure 1.2), set the puck up for defensemen, and move the puck by forechecking pressure to a waiting teammate or to an area where teammates can get the puck first. When going out to play the puck, goaltenders must check their options first and then listen to the communication of teammates in order to make the best decision. Strong, confident puckhandling goaltenders are very valuable to a team because they provide an extra breakout player and often save the defense from getting hit by the forecheckers. Also goaltenders are always facing up ice, so they see options sooner. The only problem with goaltenders handling the puck is that their passing ability is usually not as good as a defenseman's because of their restrictive equipment.

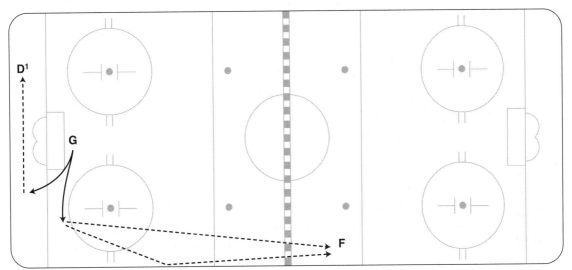

Figure 1.2   Goaltenders must learn to move the puck.

Defense

Coaches may have a different philosophy on this, but we believe the defense should be prepared to move into the breakout once a successful pass is made. Some coaches believe the defensemen should "stay at home," or always keep the play in front of them. This is a sound philosophy but significantly eliminates attack options. The key is a successful pass. The defenseman who jumps into the breakout should be the back-side D, while the puck-moving D holds a more defensive position after making the pass (figure 1.3a). The back-side D is in a better position to read the play because he is not involved in retrieving the puck and is generally waiting at the net for the play to develop. Sometimes in defensive zone coverage and in other breakout situations the center is caught low, so it is imperative that the net defenseman be ready and available for a breakout pass (figure 1.3b).

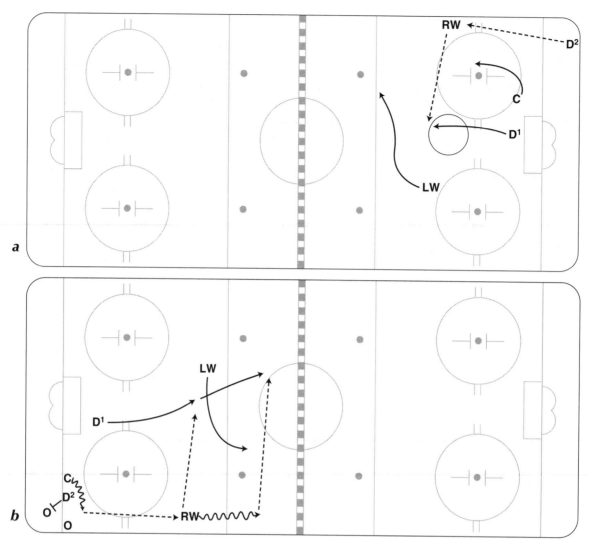

Figure 1.3   (a) The defense joining the breakout and (b) the center caught low.

In game situations it is also common to get the puck while in defensive zone coverage and then have to initiate a breakout. Using the calls "over," "up," "wheel," and "reverse," and "rim" players must read and react to the quickest escape option. Often when the defensive team recovers the puck down low, the best option is to break out by moving the puck away from pressure to the back-side D and up the other side. By breaking out on the back side, you take the puck to an area with less traffic and generally less checking pressure (figure 1.4).

Defensemen, especially young defensemen, must learn to make a strong first pass. Coaches and parents often yell to defensemen on the breakout, "Get the puck out!" What they mean is to keep the puck going up the boards or shoot it off the glass. Just do whatever you can to get the puck into the neutral zone without turning it over. At times in a game this may be the appropriate action but generally you want the defense to learn to read the play and make a tape to tape passes. It is important for defensemen to learn to make plays by picking the best option on the breakout.

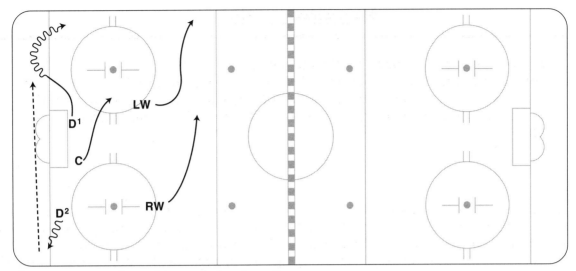

Figure 1.4   Breakout from a defensive alignment.

Sometimes the best play is an inside pass to the center or a back-side play to your partner because 80 percent of teams on the forecheck take away the boards; therefore, if you use the board option you are essentially passing into traffic and probably creating a turnover. The old saying of "never pass in front of your own net" should be thrown out the window because that is sometimes the only option, and you don't want to be predictable.

Breakout Plays

When a player goes back to break out a puck, his teammates are his number one resource. It is important that his teammates communicate pressure and also make specific calls with regard to the appropriate breakout option to use. Players can make five calls: up, over, wheel, reverse, and rim.

■ UP

When D2 calls an "up," D1 knows right away that when he touches the puck his primary option is to turn up the strong side and make a play to the board winger (LW) or center (figure 1.5). D2 has read that the other team is taking away the net or back side, so the best option is to get the puck moving right away up the strong side. C supports low, and RW moves across the ice.

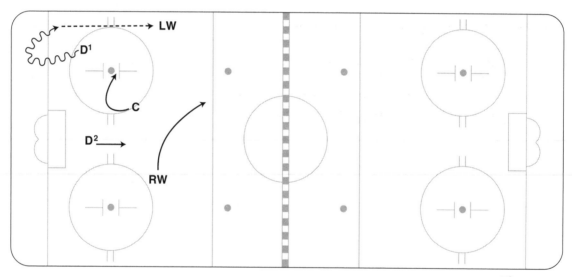

Figure 1.5

■ OVER

When D1 picks up the puck, D2 sees that the other team has flooded one side of the ice, so he moves to the opposite corner and calls for an "over" play (figure 1.6). D1 makes a direct pass or banks the puck off the boards to D2. D1 should move the puck quickly and not make the mistake of carrying the pressure toward D2 and then passing. If that were to happen, the forechecker could easily continue through and get on D2-as he receives the pass. C supports low, RW supports the boards, and LW moves across in support.

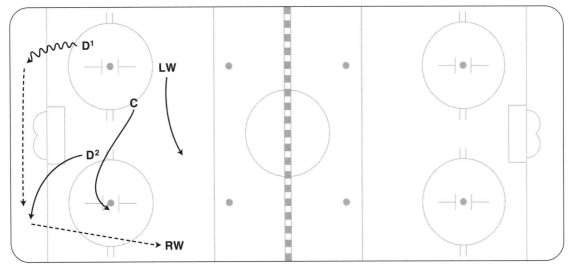

Figure 1.6

■ WHEEL

This is where D1 has a step on the forechecker, so D2 calls "wheel" and D1 quickly rounds the net, leaving the forechecker trailing. Use the net as a screen for the forechecker by cutting tight to the net on the wheel. D2 should hold the front of the net until D1 makes a play or skates up ice (figure 1.7). C supports low, LW moves across the ice, while RW provides a boards-pass option.

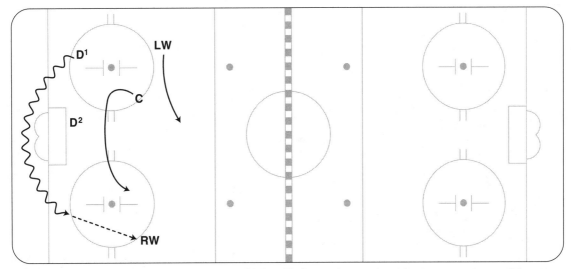

Figure 1.7

■ REVERSE

In this situation, D1 picks up the puck and attempts to lose the forechecker by going around the net. D2 sees that the forechecker is right on his partner, so he calls a reverse (figure 1.8). D1 banks the puck off the boards in behind the forechecker to D2. C supports by first moving with D1 and then back low through the slot once the reverse pass is made. LW moves inside and then out to the boards, ready for an outlet pass. RW initially is ready for the up pass from D1, and then when the reverse pass is made, RW moves across the ice to support the break-out. D2 passes to C or LW.

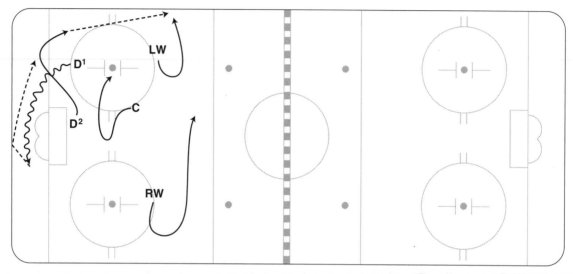

Figure 1.8

Sometimes coaches like the center and the winger to switch on reverse plays, which allows them to maintain speed—teams must make sure the exchange is done quickly so they don't give up defensive position at a time when a turnover may occur. As noted in figure 1.9, when D1 swings behind the net, C moves to support. If D1 reverses the puck, C can continue moving toward the boards, and RW can move to mid-ice to support the reverse pass to D2.

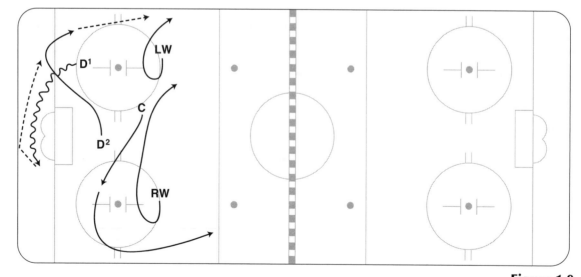

Figure 1.9

The final option for reverse plays is for D1 to reverse the puck to C in the strong-side corner. This allows the breakout team to spread out and makes it difficult for the forecheckers to take away all options. D2 supports the wide side, looking for an over pass, and D1 reverses the puck to C, who should call this option.

■ RIM

This option (figure 1.10) is often used when the opposition is forechecking hard and the best choice is to bypass the forecheck by passing the puck hard around the boards. D1 goes back for the puck and quickly rims the puck to RW. C supports from underneath, and LW moves across in support. Against teams who pinch down with their defense on rimmed pucks, the wingers who receive the rim must be able to protect the puck, control it, and then move it to support. In this situation, RW must be able to control the puck and make a play, skate with the puck, or chip it behind the pinching defenseman. As mentioned earlier, the ability to get pucks off the boards under pressure is a skill that also involves a component of toughness—especially if the other team's defensemen pinch down quickly to finish the hit.

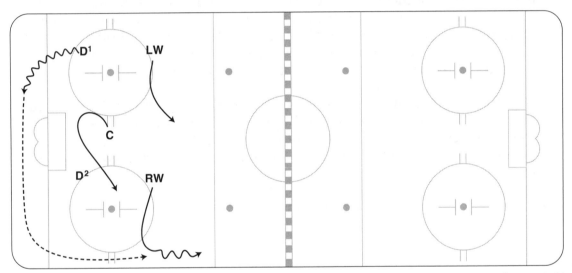

Figure 1.10

Control Breakouts

There are times when your team gets the puck and the opposing players have already pulled back into a trap forecheck. They are back toward the neutral zone waiting for the breakout to take place and looking to turn the puck over. Instead of freelancing your way through the trap and many times being unsuccessful, it is better to move out together in a coordinated fashion. This is called a control breakout.

Unless you come out of your zone in a controlled manner with set patterns for the five players, it is too easy for the opponent to create a turnover. There are two key factors in a controlled breakout: (1) the four players without the puck move with speed, and (2) the puck carrier knows the options and picks the best one. In a control setup, the puck carrier is like a quarterback who knows the routes of the receivers and picks which option is open. This section includes diagrams of three control breakouts where the effect of moving in a coordinated fashion will provide you with enough options to break the trap. They are all equally successful, but it is difficult to learn and execute all three, so coaches should pick one and practice it over and over until it becomes automatic. Often when these breakouts are run effectively, they not only result in breaking the trap but also generate a scoring chance.

In all control breakout situations, the idea is to give the defenseman with the puck more options than the opposition can take away. It is up to the defenseman to make the right choice, but the coaching staff must also prepare the team for specific options that may work against certain opponents.

■ BLUE-TO-BLUE STRETCH

D1 waits behind the net for C to move back with speed. C swings with speed behind the net. D2 swings into the opposite corner. LW waits at the corner of the close blue line. RW waits at the corner of the far blue line. There are four options available to D1. C can pick up the puck with speed and try to weave his way through the trap or move the puck to LW, RW, or back to D1 and up the other side (figure 1.11a). D1 can allow C to go through and then step out the other side of the net and pass to LW or D2 (figure 1.11b). If D1 passes to D2, the next primary option should be a stretch pass to RW moving across the ice or to LW, who bends his pattern through the center of the ice.

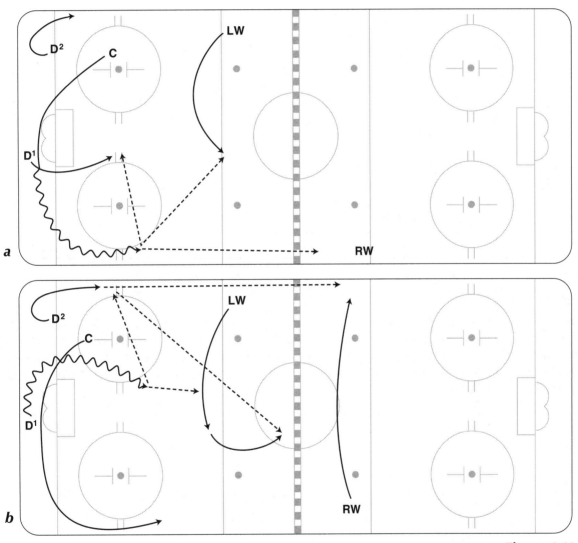

Figure 1.11

■ STRONG-SIDE SLANT

D1 waits behind the net for C to swing. C can swing behind the net or into the far corner. RW swings on the same side but a bit higher up than C. LW stations himself at center ice along the boards. D2 waits deep in the corner. D1 now passes to D2, who then has three options as he moves up ice: (1) Pass to LW, who can pass or chip the puck to RW as he slants across mid-ice; (2) pass to RW; (3) pass across to the center on the far side. The key players are RW and C as they move with speed to break through the trap (figure 1.12).

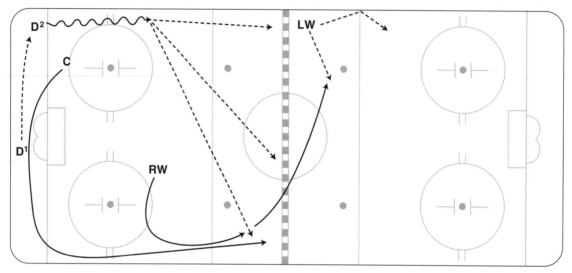

Figure 1.12

■ THREE HIGH

D1 waits behind the net for a few seconds. All three forwards stay out high in the neutral zone. D2 supports D1 by moving wide into one of the corners. D1 steps out and passes to C curling in mid-ice or to LW or RW, who are moving or posting up (stationary along the boards by one of the lines). If C is under pressure when he receives the puck, he may chip it by and create a footrace for LW or RW (figure 1.13).

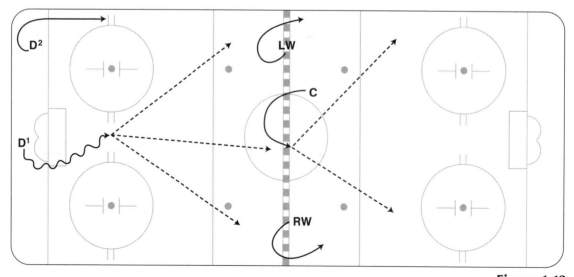

Figure 1.13

Chapter 2

Neutral Zone Counters and Regroups

For the purpose of clarity, this section deals with plays that originate in the neutral zone as opposed to plays that originate in the defensive zone and move through the neutral zone. There are basically two types of attacks that involve the neutral zone: (1) the rush, which is a continuation of the breakout, or (2) regroups and counters. All rush plays are covered in the next chapter on offensive zone entries. This chapter focuses on transition plays such as quick counters and regroups. Puck possession in the neutral zone usually results from a turnover or face-off. When the defensive team gets the puck off a turnover, it is important to move through the neutral zone quickly and catch the opposition behind the play. Advancing the puck through the neutral zone off a face-off is more challenging because the opposing players are initially aligned above the puck. Although the neutral zone is technically between the blue lines, we have expanded this area to include the tops of the circles at the attacking team's end in order to allow the play to develop (figure 2.1).

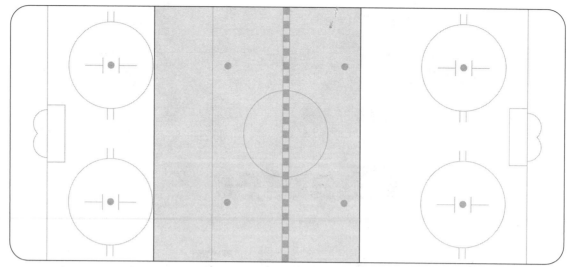

Figure 2.1   The neutral zone.

Counters

The difference between counters and regroups is that counters require speed while regroups are more controlled. A team wants to counter quickly when the opponent isn't set up in a neutral zone forecheck. Quick counters often result in odd-man rushes. When the turnover happens, the opposition is moving aggressively on the attack and often cannot react quickly enough to get back. This is why it is important to practice counters with speed. When a team counters, the intent is to catch the opponent moving toward the offensive zone and then quickly pass the puck up to the forwards and hopefully get an odd-man rush. If this happens 50 percent of the time, then your team would be considered a very good transition team. The other 50 percent of the time the pass is confronted by pressure, and the puck carrier must look for a play or dump the puck into the offensive zone.

Practice repetition will help teach defensemen to read the forecheck and then pick the appropriate option. There are times when players counter quickly but then the puck carrier is confronted or runs out of space to carry the puck, which leaves the player with only two options: either dump the puck in or chip behind pressure.

Dump-Ins

Dumping the puck in is one counter option when players are confronted. Some teams like to designate where to always dump the puck so that skaters off the puck will know which area to move toward. There are four options for players when dumping the puck.

1. **Cross-corner dump-in:** This is effective because it forces the defensive team to switch coverage from one side of the ice to the other, and in

doing so they may lose defensive position. Effective cross-corner dumps also give the offensive team a chance to get to the puck first. Make sure when dumping the puck that it does not move into the area where the goaltender can play it. Try to dead corner it by placing it in the corner so it stops there (figure 2.2).

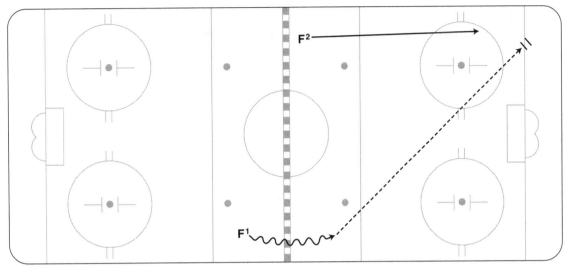

Figure 2.2   Cross-corner dump-in.

2. **Hard, wide rim:** The puck carrier shoots the puck into the zone so that it rims around the boards and comes up the wide side for the wide winger to retrieve (figure 2.3). Make sure it is hard enough so that the goaltender cannot stop it behind the net. This will be a difficult puck for the winger to get off the boards, so he should stop it first then protect it and look for a play. As in the previous strategy, quickly changing sides with the puck usually results in the defensive team losing their position in the zone when they adjust to the puck.

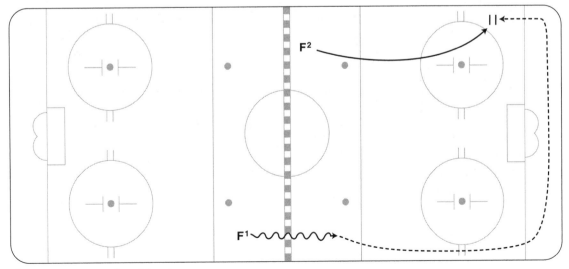

Figure 2.3   Hard, wide rim.

3. **Same-side dump-in:** Much like the cross-corner dump, the intent of this strategy is to have the puck stop in the near corner (figure 2.4). When pressured in the neutral zone, the puck carrier lays the puck behind pressure by shooting it into the near corner for a supporting teammate. Most opposing defensemen will try to stay up on the puck carrier, which will allow the supporting offensive forward to get to the puck first. Often with a same-side dump, the puck carrier has enough speed that he can jump around the defenseman and get to the puck first.

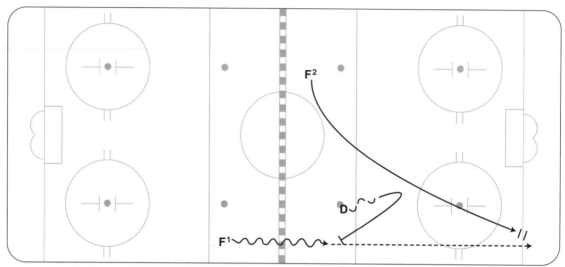

Figure 2.4   Same-side dump-in.

4. **Putting the puck on net:** When watching sports highlights, you will often see a player skating through the neutral zone, faking a dump-in to the corner, and then surprising the goaltender by shooting the puck on net (figure 2.5). At times it will go in, but this is rare. The strategy is that it catches the goaltender by surprise and forces him to make a play. Many goalies have trouble stick handling and passing the puck, so this tactic often forces the opposing defensemen to hurry back and receive a below-average pass from the goaltender to start the breakout. If the goaltender you are playing against is a weak passer, this option may be a good strategy. Also, some shots are hard for goaltenders to handle, so they simply direct the puck into the corner, which makes for a very difficult play for the defensemen. They have to retrieve the puck and then turn around and make a play while under heavy forechecking pressure. Most of the time when a rebound is created by a long shot on goal, the offensive team has as good a chance of recovering the puck as the defensive team.

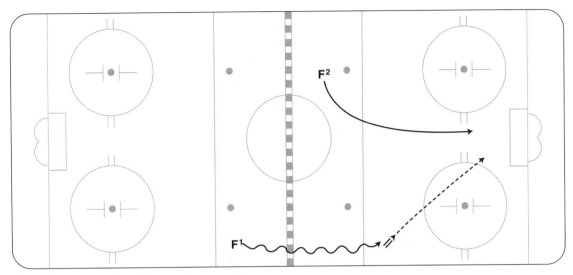

Figure 2.5　Putting the puck on net.

Odd-Man Rushes and Breakaways

Dumping the puck into the zone is an effective strategy, but the more exciting transition play—and the one that usually results in a scoring chance—involves the defensive team getting the puck in the neutral zone and making a penetrating pass to one of the forwards that results in an odd-man rush or breakaway (figure 2.6). There are two key aspects of this counter play: (1) the defenseman recognizes the option quickly, and (2) the forward skates into a stretch area with timing and speed. The stretch area is an open space as far away from the puck carrier as a skater can go without going offside.

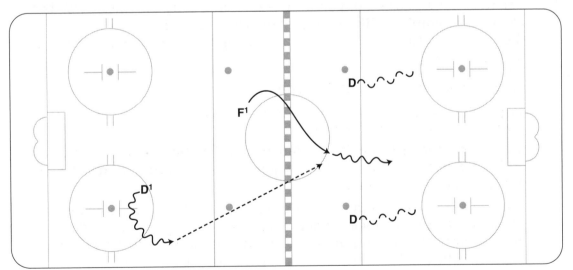

Figure 2.6　Making a penetrating pass for an odd-man rush or breakaway.

Sometimes the forward off the puck can get in behind the defense and look for that breakaway pass (figure 2.7). This option will be available more often against teams that pinch up in the neutral zone with their defense.

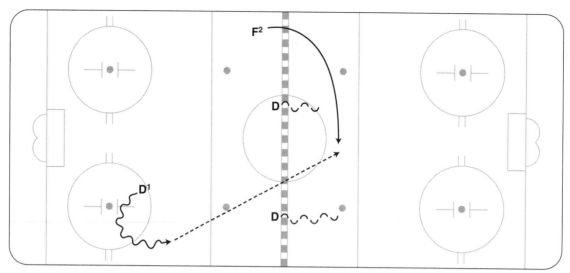

Figure 2.7   Getting open behind the Ds for a breakaway pass.

Forwards can look for that high middle area between the opposing defensemen to open up. When his teammate is ready to pass he should move to that area quickly with good timing. Even if the pass isn't made, having the forward available will pull back the opposing defensemen and open up other areas. Now that the red line has been removed for offside passes, it is a good strategy to have one forward stretch in all counter situations.

The other factor to consider when executing neutral zone counters is involving the defense in the attack. In most North American leagues it is very difficult to generate offense, and that is why coaches should look for ways to get their defense involved. It doesn't have to be all the time, but it is a strategy that your team must practice and use according to your need to generate more scoring opportunities. Relying only on the forwards to score limits a team's ability to be a dangerous offensive unit.

There are several advantages to activating your defensemen through the neutral zone:

O It gives you one more passing option.

O It provides the defensive team with one more player to cover, often confusing their defensive system.

O It prepares the attack to have a late or mid-ice threat from the defense. If the defensemen wait too long to join the attack, they won't be a factor in the offensive zone.

O Having a defenseman in the play often backs off the opposing defense, therefore giving the puck carrier more time to skate or make a decision. It is important to note that defensemen cannot jump indiscriminately into an attack. The decision to activate must always be based on the quality of puck possession. If the puck carrier has good possession, then the defenseman can move to become an option; if not, he should stay back.

Here are three ways that defensemen can activate on counters.

■ BACK-SIDE OPTION

In this situation, the defenseman sees the pass being made on the strong side and jumps up the back side to look for a pass or enter the zone as a late option (figure 2.8). When seeing D2 activate, D1 must move to a mid-ice position in case of a breakdown.

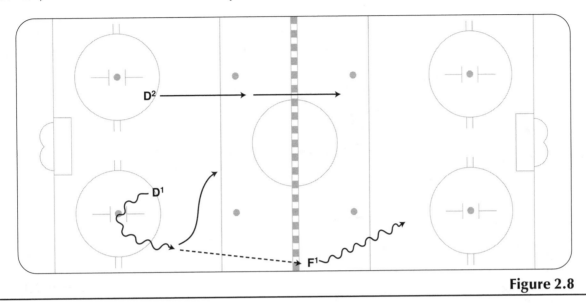

Figure 2.8

■ PASS AND GO

Here the defenseman recognizes after he passes up the strong side that the forward will need an option right away, so he moves into the opening for a potential inside play (figure 2.9). When seeing D1 activate, D2 must stay in mid-ice and behind the play.

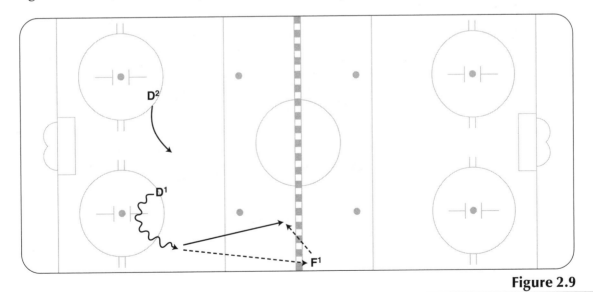

Figure 2.9

■ MID-ICE TWO ON ONE

When the center gets the puck low, the opposite D can move in through mid-ice and create a close support option for the puck carrier (figure 2.10). D2 remains back and in mid-ice in case of a turnover.

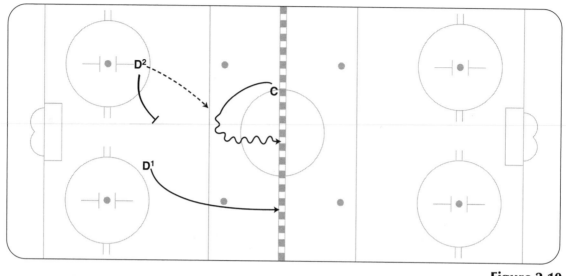

Figure 2.10

Regroups

If the opponents are already set up and in position to forecheck in the neutral zone, then regroups are a more effective way to break through this area and enter the offensive zone. Most teams will have a set forecheck in the neutral zone to try to prevent teams from successfully regrouping. It is important to know before you play a team which forecheck they are using—this will help identify what regroup options are available. The coach must decide for all regroups what patterns the forwards should run, so they are consistent. This will help the defense identify where potential passing options may exist because the forwards are available in consistent areas. The two regroup patterns we will discuss are lane regroups and motion regroups. Both regroups are effective against all types of forechecking pressure. The difference in the two is whether the center stays in the middle or does he have the freedom to swing wide and exchange with the wingers (figure 2.11a).

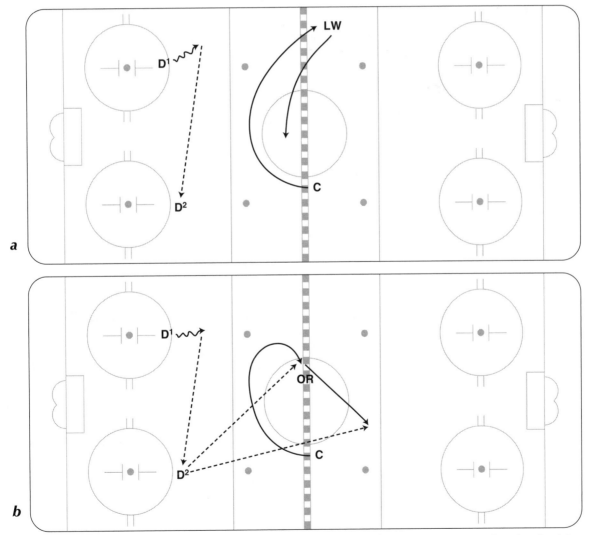

Figure 2.11   *(a)* Center exchanging with the winger; *(b)* Center supporting both sides (low/high).

Lane Regroups

For the following regroups, the strong-side forward supports the boards while the back-side forward stretches. The center supports both sides, either low or high (figure 2.11*b*). The sequence of options for defensemen in the neutral zone depends on how the opponents forecheck. Do they forecheck with two forwards in a 2-1-2 system or with one forward in a 1-2-2 or 1-3-1 setup? If they forecheck with one forward, does he take away the D-to-D pass, or does he take away the flat pass to the wide forward? Teams that take away the D-to-D pass eliminate the hinge play, while teams that take away the cross-ice pass give up the hinge play. These are important reads that help the defensemen choose which of the following options to use.

■ QUICK UP

In this situation, D1 gets the puck just inside the blue line and turns it up quickly by passing to LW or C (figure 2.12). This should be the first option for all teams because speed in transition usually results in odd-man rushes, plus the quick-up play does not give the opposition time to set up a trap. RW stretches on the wide side and then supports across the ice when the pass is made.

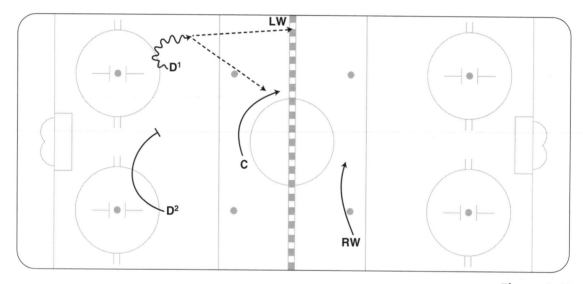

Figure 2.12

■ D-TO-D STRETCH

When D1 gets the puck and the strong-side options are taken away, then he should immediately pass the puck to his partner (figure 2.13). Once the pass is made, D1 should sink back to mid-ice to protect his partner in case of a turnover and also to provide an option for D2. D2 passes up to RW, who is in a stretch position by the far blue line, or to C in mid-ice. Once the pass is made the LW moves to support.

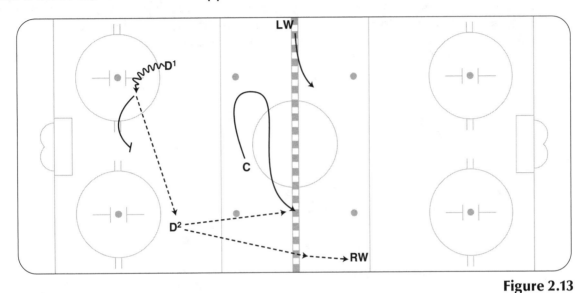

Figure 2.13

■ D-TO-D FLAT PASS

D1 passes to D2, and now the opposition takes away his options to RW and C. D2 passes across to LW, who sinks low into the open seam (figure 2.14). This option is usually available when the opponents forecheck in a 1-2-2 format and lock the center leaving the back side open. When D2 initially gets the pass from D1 he should move up ice and look to make a play up the boards or to the center. This deception will open up the wide side to LW. The pass must be made flat across the ice because a diagonal pass might be intercepted.

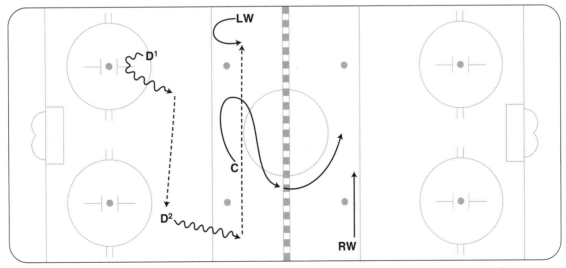

Figure 2.14

■ HINGE PLAY

D1 passes to D2 and then slides back to mid-ice to support his partner (figure 2.15a). D2 moves up ice and looks to make a pass. With no option available, he passes back to D1, who is behind and in mid-ice. D1 then moves the puck quickly to LW as the primary option or to C. Initially when D1 moves the puck to D2, he has the option to drop back deeper and perform a skating hinge—this is where the supporting defenseman moves back in behind the play and prepares to jump into the hinge pass with speed, catching the opponent off guard. Using the skating hinge also gives this defenseman room to accelerate, time to read the play, and the ability to draw in a checker and move the puck to the best option (figure 2.15b).

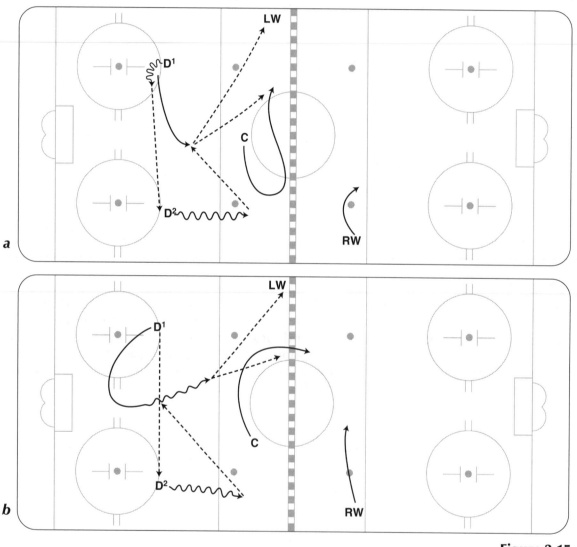

Figure 2.15

CENTER STRETCH

When a D1-to-D2 pass is made in the neutral zone, C should support low, but once the puck is passed back to D1 or LW, C should have the option of returning low or moving into the high mid-ice stretch area (figure 2.16) for a potential breakaway pass. If teams check center on center in the neutral zone, this is an effective way to lose your check and split the opponent's defense.

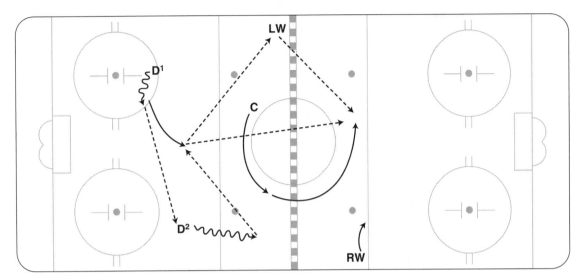

Figure 2.16

CHIP BEHIND PRESSURE

Because most teams use tight-checking systems, there isn't a lot of room in the neutral zone. When a pass is made to a teammate in this area, it is important that the receiver have quick and close support. If the pass receiver is confronted, he will now have the option of chipping the puck into the space behind the checker. The support player can anticipate this and get to the puck first. This is very effective if the pass is confronted by the opposing defenseman stepping up to make a hit. In most cases, the center should be the player who is ready to support the chip (figure 2.17).

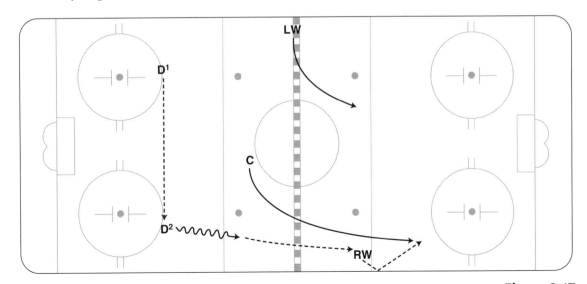

Figure 2.17

DEFENSE SUPPORTING MID-ICE

When a pass is made by a defenseman to a forward in the neutral zone, the passing D should be ready to move up through mid-ice and support the attack (figure 2.18). As the partner of D1, D2 must remain in a strong center-ice position behind the attack. D1 must again read the quality of puck possession to determine how far to move up and how quickly.

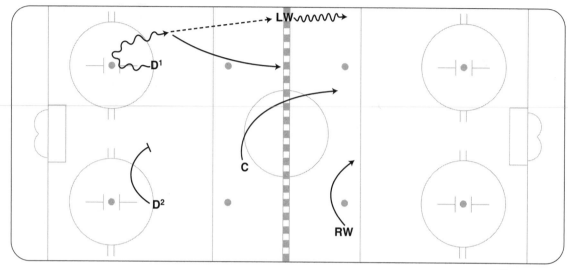

Figure 2.18

Motion Regroups

The difference with motion regroups is that the center now has the ability to exchange positions with the wingers. Once again, the sequence of options for defensemen in the neutral zone depends on how the opponents forecheck. The advantage of using motion regroups is that the players have more speed when getting the pass and often catch the opposition flat footed. The disadvantage is that the positioning of the forwards is not as predictable and as a result the defensemen can't always anticipate where they will be. At times the forwards are so focused on moving and building up speed that they lose eye contact with the passer. The forwards must remember to keep their eyes on the puck. With motion regroups, the center always changes lanes with one of the wingers, and then that winger moves into center ice. If the player in the middle moves to support a pass and it is not made, an exchange occurs with the winger on that side (figure 2.19a). The player in the center may also swing away to build up speed on the wide side (figure 2.19b).

With motion regroups, if teams check center on center in the neutral zone, having the center move into an outside lane often results in coverage confusion.

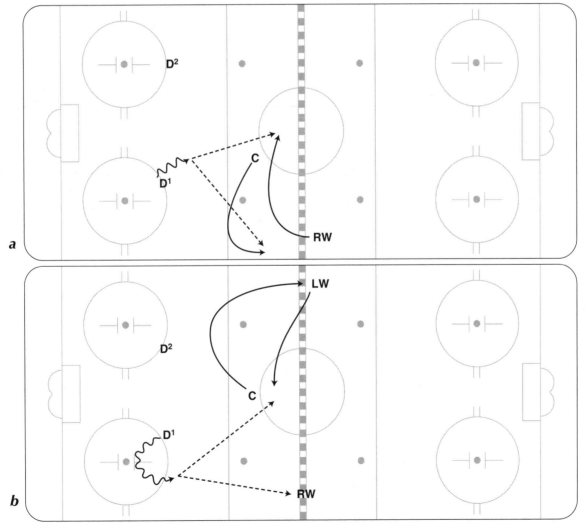

Figure 2.19   *(a)* Strong-side motion regroup and *(b)* the wide-side motion regroup.

Using the same options presented for lane regroups, we now look at how the passing options change with the center leaving the mid-ice lane.

■ QUICK UP

In this situation, D1 gets the puck just inside the blue line and turns it up quickly by passing to LW or RW, who has moved off the wide boards as C swings to that side (figure 2.20). The exchange between the center and RW must be made quickly in order to provide immediate support for D1.

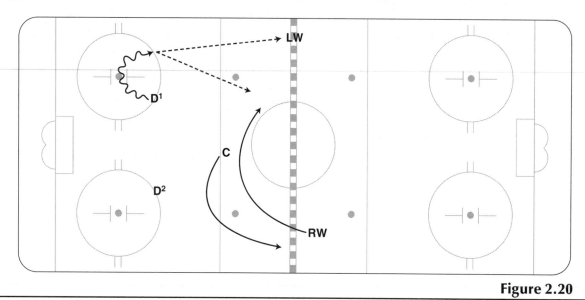

Figure 2.20

■ D-TO-D STRETCH

When D1 gets the puck and the strong-side options are taken away, he then passes to his partner (figure 2.21). C once again swings away to the wide side. Once the pass is made, D1 should sink back to mid-ice to protect his partner in case of a turnover and also to provide an option for D2. D2 passes up to RW or to LW who has moved off the boards and is available in the middle of the ice.

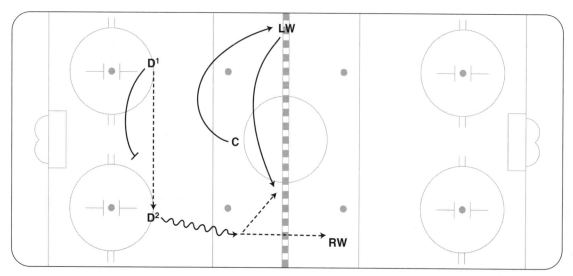

Figure 2.21

■ D-TO-D FLAT PASS

D1 passes to D2, and now because of how the opponents are forechecking, the main option is to make a flat pass to C with speed in the wide lane (figure 2.22). This is one of the more effective options in the motion regroup sequence because the center tends to build up a lot of speed in the wide lane and can often enter the zone easily. This option is usually available when the opponents forecheck in a 1-2-2 formation and lock the center of the ice, leaving the back side open.

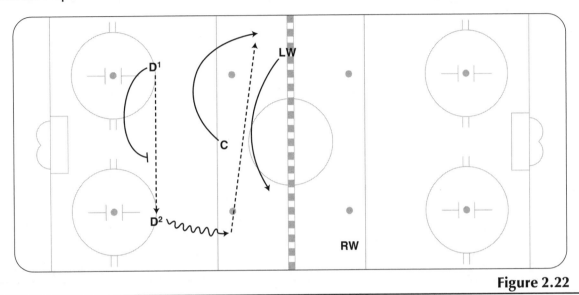

Figure 2.22

■ HINGE PLAY

D1 passes to D2 and then slides back to mid-ice to support his partner. D2 moves up ice and looks to make a pass. With no option available, he passes back to D1, who is behind and in mid-ice. D1 then moves the puck quickly to C, who once again has a lot of speed built up in the outside lane (figure 2.23). LW may also be available in the middle of the ice. D1 may perform a skating hinge and accelerate up the middle of the ice while looking for options.

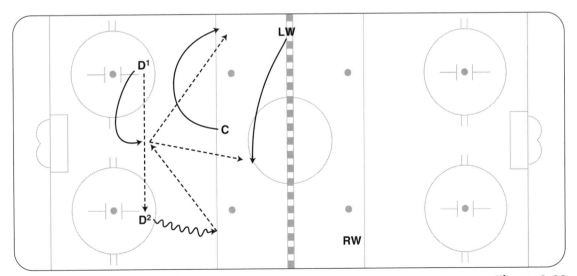

Figure 2.23

■ STRETCH PASS

When a D1-to-D2 pass is made in the neutral zone, C exchanges with the wing, and now RW has the option of moving out higher in behind the opposing defense (figure 2.24). Because the center swings lower, this provides the defense with an alternative safer option if the stretch play is not there. The RW must time it to hit the open space behind the opposition defense when D2 is ready to pass.

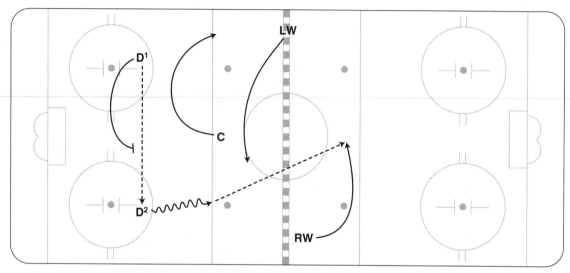

Figure 2.24

Chapter 3
Offensive Zone Entries

I n this chapter, we deal with plays entering the offensive zone. Whether the rush starts from a successful breakout in the defensive zone or results from a counter or regroup in the neutral zone, offensive zone entry is a key strategy for generating successful scoring chances.

Entering the offensive zone in control of the puck is every player's goal. Not turning the puck over when entering the offensive zone is every coach's goal. Let's face it. We play this game to battle for and enjoy possession of the puck. Puck possession needs to be a key underlying philosophy, not only for playing hockey at a high level but also for its enjoyment.

Coaches universally get disappointed with players who needlessly lose possession of the puck in two areas. The first is the 7 or 8 feet (2.1 or 2.4 m) just outside the blue line, and the second is the 7 or 8 feet (2.1 or 2.4 m) just inside the blue line. Players turning over pucks in these two critical areas tend to hear about it. Why? When the puck is turned over here, the opposing team can counter quickly and create outnumbered attacks. This happens because the two forwards without the puck tend to be anticipating the puck going deep, and they are in that "flat" vulnerable position along the blue line with no speed (figure 3.1).

When playing five on five, a player with the puck wide entering the offensive zone must read the opponent's pressure. If the gap between the player with the puck and the defender is large or adequate, obviously the attacking player keeps possession of the puck and enters the attacking zone. If the player with the puck senses pressure, then the cross-ice dump or chip are two tactics used to reduce this pressure and ensure a chance for puck possession deeper in the zone. Coaches should set up practice drills which incorporate this read. Drills which allow the puck carrier to react to varying gaps by the defender and also varying pressure; all help to make these decisions with the puck more automatic and successful in game action.

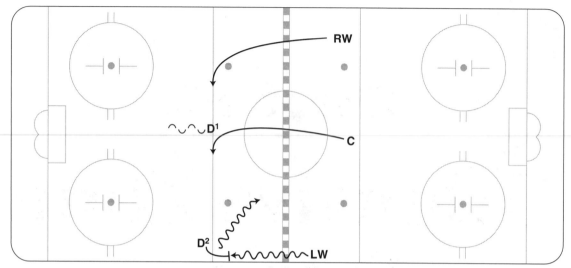

Figure 3.1   Turnover at the blue line.

Dump-In Entries

The cross-ice dump (figure 3.2) works best under two conditions:

1. Defensive pressure is read, and the offensive team is changing.
2. Defensive pressure is read, and an offensive support player is skating in the wide lane.

   The perfect cross-ice dump hits the boards halfway between the net and the side boards and angles away from the goalie toward the half boards.

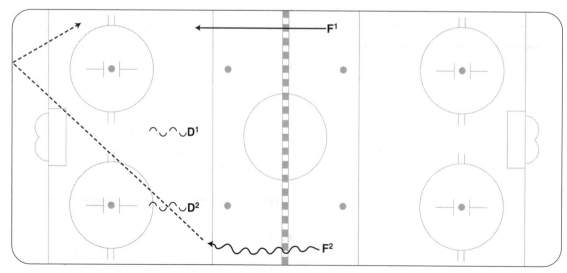

Figure 3.2   The cross-ice dump-in.

Rims

A second tactic when the offensive player with possession of the puck reads pressure is the rim. The player entering the zone senses that his teammate skating wide can retrieve the puck, and therefore the player with the puck rims it hard around the boards (figure 3.3). At the very top levels of the game of hockey, this tactic has limited success. Goalies in today's game are so mobile and so good at trapping the rimmed puck that very few pucks get around to the desired teammate. Most are stopped behind the net and turned over to the opposing defense. Before using this tactic know the opposition goaltender and if he is not mobile or is poor at trapping the puck off a rim, then use it more often. Conversely if he gets out of his net quick and is able to handle the puck then dumping it in will only result in a turnover.

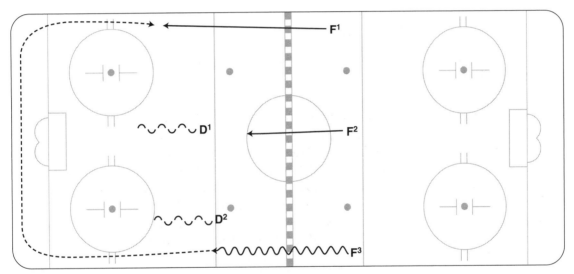

Figure 3.3   The basic rim.

Chips

The chip tactic (figure 3.4) is used in many different areas of the ice but may be most effective during an offensive zone entry. Chipping the puck refers to banking the puck off the boards to a space behind the defender. The chip works so well because it puts the puck in better offensive position (behind the pressuring defender) and also gives the player chipping the puck a good chance of retrieving it. Younger players make a monumental mistake by not pulling the defender off the boards slightly toward the middle of the ice before chipping the puck. If players are close to or right next to the boards, it is nearly impossible to angle the chip to a place where it can be retrieved. The goal of the chip is puck placement. Chipping the puck past the defender now forces him to turn and try to catch the offensive player. Because the offensive player is moving forward with speed and his supporting teammates are also moving to that area the defender is often caught in a difficult position. Several years ago the defender would have been able to hook or hold up the offensive player for a few seconds but not anymore . . . the obstruction rules have eliminated that tactic. Therefore the defender's inability to pressure the player with the puck and creates the opportunity for puck possession deeper in the offensive zone.

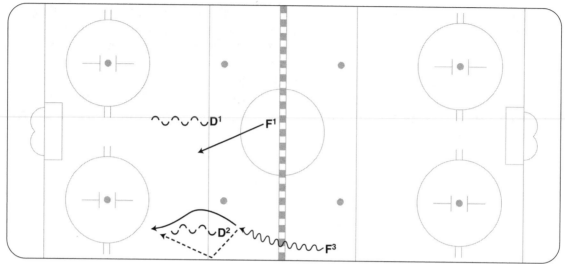

Figure 3.4   The basic chip.

The chip has two options for retrieval. The first is to chip the puck and have the same player retrieve it. The second and most effective is to chip the puck into the space behind the defenseman and have a teammate with speed pick it up (figure 3.5). The chip to a teammate should always be used when the puck carrier has no room to carry the puck but has a teammate moving to support the space behind the defense. This strategy is also commonly referred to as attacking the space behind the opposing defense. Get your players to visualize this tactic and constantly talk about the "space behind".

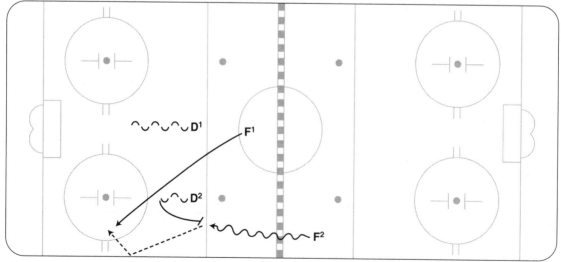

Figure 3.5   Chipping the puck behind the defenseman to a teammate.

Mid-Ice Entries

Most coaches prefer outside-drive entries because there is usually less chance for a dangerous turnover. Players who enter the offensive zone with the puck in the middle of the ice face several risks. The major concern is that any sideways movement in the middle of the ice brings with it the opportunity for the defenseman to stand up and make an open-ice hit. Most major (Scott Stevens or Dion Phaneuf–like) open-ice hits occur as players are carrying the puck into the middle of the ice on offensive zone entries (figure 3.6).

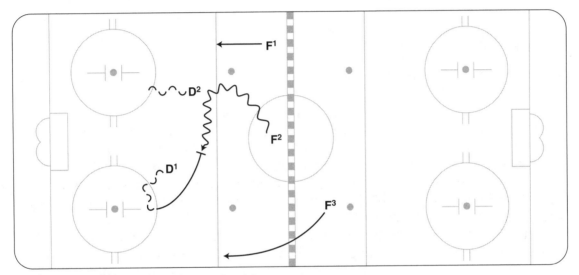

Figure 3.6   Mid-ice entry open-ice hit.

Many talented and offensively gifted players use this middle-ice space to pass off to teammates coming from behind the play with speed. This entry tactic is exceptional when executed properly because backspeed—players moving from behind the puck carrier with more speed than the puck carrier—can completely catch defenders off guard.

The back-side pass upon middle entry (figure 3.7) is the most difficult to execute because it requires more skill, but it is always the most effective. Players gifted with the puck often carry it across the middle of the offensive zone just inside the blue line and then pass back toward the space where they have just come from to a player with vertical speed. The effectiveness of this entry comes from shifting the defenders sideways, with the puck carrier thereby opening up space for the player on the back side to enter the zone.

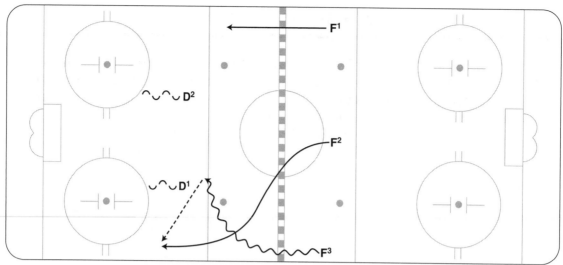

Figure 3.7 Mid-ice entry back-side pass.

A second option for the puck carrier in mid-ice (F1) is to drive across the line through the middle and then bump the puck to the outside player stationary at the blue line (F2). As F1 continues to drive to the net, this will free up space and time for F2 to shoot or make a play. F2 will have the option to shoot with F1 screening the goaltender, pass across to F3, or hit the late D1 moving in. If there are no options available, then F2 can lay the puck behind the net to F1 for low puck possession. This "ladder play" is one of the most effective plays for drawing the defense in tight as F1 enters the zone then pushing them back as F1 passes off and drives to the net. It definitely creates a lot of defensive coverage confusion (figure 3.8).

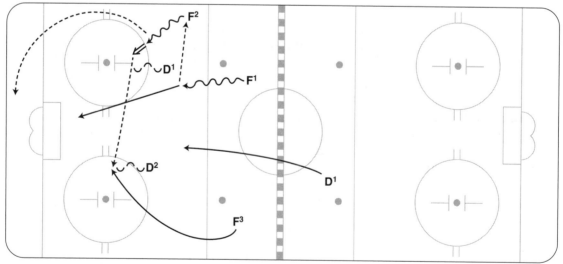

Figure 3.8 Midlane ladder play.

Wide-Lane Drives

The wide-lane drive is the most utilized offensive zone entry because this is the space most often available to the puck carrier. When the puck carrier enters the zone wide, he may have the option to drive deep and try to go around the defenseman or behind the net. Defensemen are usually intimidated by speed and want to protect the space inside, so they will initially give the puck carrier room on the outside and then try to cut the puck carrier off deeper in the zone. The puck carrier may also delay by driving deep and then cutting back up ice or driving and cutting inside. It is important to read options quickly as you enter the zone wide with speed. The puck carrier going wide needs to read where the open space is—if it is deep then drive around the defenseman; if it is in front then cut laterally across in front of the defenseman; if the defenseman closes quickly on the puck carrier then the best option may be to spin off and delay (figure 3.9).

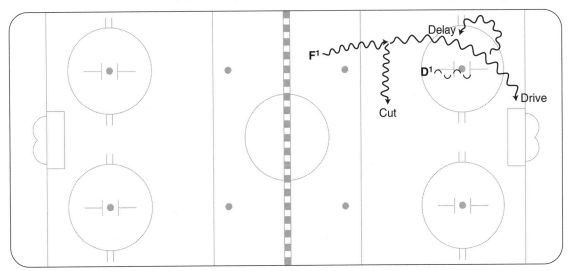

Figure 3.9 The wide-lane drive with options to cut, drive deep, or delay.

The Funnel

Sometimes coaches need to have in their back pockets a tactic or philosophy that simplifies the offense into a couple of simple ideas. The funnel (figure 3.10) is one of these. Many coaches like the funnel because its main emphasis is to get pucks to the net through traffic. The funnel philosophy says that once a player carrying the puck crosses the top of the offensive face-off circles, that player has only one option: placing the puck toward the front of the net. Under these instructions, the other two offensive forwards should not be trying to get open for a pass but should be driving hard to the net looking for a second-chance rebound. In other words, everything—the puck and the players—gets funneled toward the front of the net. If 70 to 80 percent of all goals scored come off of a second chance created by a rebound, then the funnel simplifies how to make this happen. In every league the leading scorers are the ones who take the most shots. They understand the funnel philosophy—get the puck to the net. Volume of shots is key.

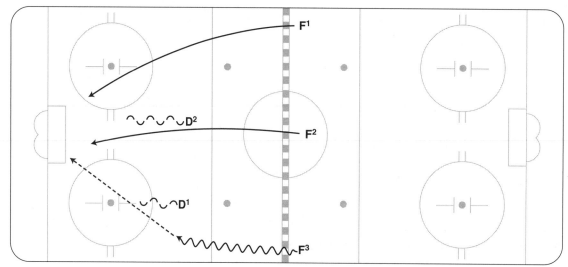

Figure 3.10   The funnel.

The funnel opportunity gets maximized if the player carrying the puck into the offensive zone and placing the puck toward the front of the net is an offensive defenseman (figure 3.11). Obviously, this frees up all three offensive forwards to skate into prime position and jump on any loose pucks to create second shots. When shooting from the outside players should recognize that they aren't trying to score. At most levels the goaltending is too good and few are beat from these wide angles. The main objective is to hit the net and create a rebound for the players going to the net.

Therefore shoot low for the wide pad and 90% of the time a rebound will come out into the slot. It is very difficult for any goaltender to deflect this type of shot to the outside.

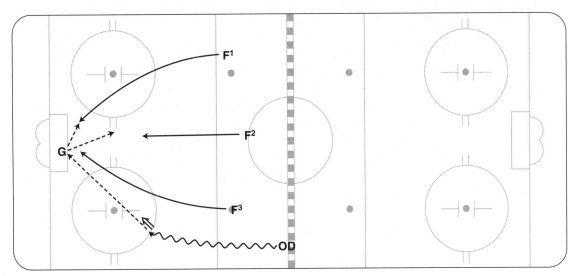

Figure 3.11   The funnel with an offensive defenseman.

The funnel play is also a simple way to activate the mid-ice defenseman. If the defenseman on the rush has speed to attack the net off the rush, then many coaches give the attacking defenseman permission to attack the front of the net, with one rule—once the play turns from a rush to a forecheck, the attacking defenseman must return quickly and directly to the blue line. Another simple rule for the offensive defenseman joining the rush or joining the attack is the function of time. Many coaches prefer that their defensemen not join the rush or the attack with minutes to go in the period or the game, especially if the team is winning by a certain margin.

Two-on-One Attacks

When the offensive team realizes they have a potential two-on-one opportunity in the neutral zone, they should attack quickly with speed (figure 3.12). Initially they may cross, but it is important to attack with speed so that the backcheckers don't catch them and nullify the odd-man rush. If it is a wide two on one, players should try to get closer to mid-ice right away. Regardless of what side the puck carrier is on once he crosses the blue line he should get the puck into a triple-threat position. A triple threat position is when the puck carrier keeps the puck at his side in shooting position so that he can either pass, shoot, or make a move. The puck carrier now needs to read how the defense and goaltender might play the situation and pick the best option. The second offensive player must have his stick in a position to shoot or deflect the puck into the net.

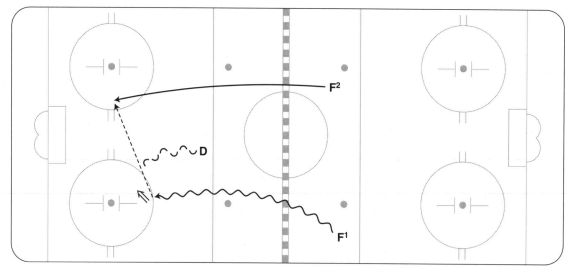

Figure 3.12   A two-on-one attack.

Two-on-Two Attacks

There are basically three strategies for a two-on-two rush. There are no set rules when to use each but they give the offensive players options. Sometimes the choice will be made by the coaches' philosophy of play but regardless it will be important to practice each option. The key principle for all two-on-two rushes is for the offensive players to isolate the attack on one of the defenders.

■ TWO-ON-TWO CRISSCROSS

The first strategy is for the puck carrier (F1) to crisscross with F2 and isolate one of the defensemen (figure 3.13). If properly executed, the crisscross creates a lateral move that develops a sense of uncertainty in the defender's mind. The key to the crisscross is for the player with the puck to initiate the lateral movement and be closest to the defenders; the player without the puck crosses in the opposite direction behind the puck carrier. Young players often mess up this sequence and put themselves offside because the player without the puck is too anxious and goes ahead of the puck carrier. Allow the puck carrier to make a decision as to which way he will go.

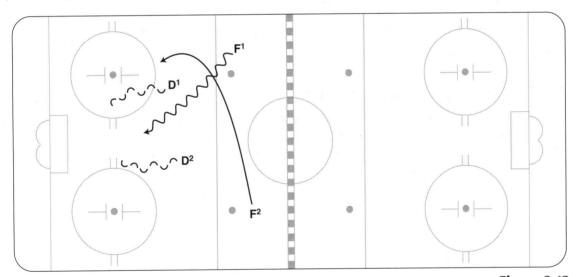

Figure 3.13

■ TWO-ON-TWO MIDLANE DRIVE

The second option for the two on two is for the player off the puck (F2) to drive through the middle of the two defensemen, allowing F1 to cross in behind (figure 3.14). This must be executed just inside the blue line so that the player without the puck doesn't go offside. Driving between the two defensemen creates a brief hesitation by the defenseman playing F1. This hesitation by the defender will allow F1 time and space to cross and shoot or make a play.

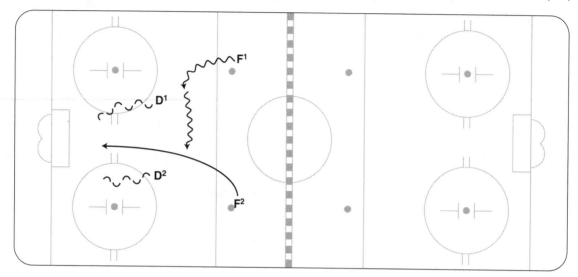

Figure 3.14

■ TWO-ON-TWO DOUBLE DRIVE

The third option is for both players to double drive. F1 may lay the puck to F2 in the space behind the defender. F2 must move to that space on the inside shoulder of the defending defenseman (D2) (figure 3.15). With the double drive, F1 might choose to shoot off the drive as F2 goes to the net for a rebound.

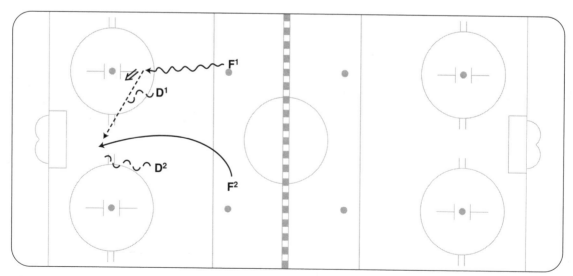

Figure 3.15

Three-on-Two Attacks

When you catch the opposition in a three on two, you should be able to generate a scoring chance. Although obviously not as good as a two on one, it is still a great offensive opportunity. Because three players are involved in the attack, several options are available to create that great chance. Teams should practice and utilize all four attack options: the high triangle, the midlane drive, the triple drive, and the drive and delay.

■ THREE-ON-TWO HIGH TRIANGLE

Let's start with the traditional option. Most often in three-on-two situations, the attacking team wants to force the defenders to play man on man with one player and isolate the other defender two on one. F1 drives wide with the puck, and F3 drives wide without the puck. F2 now trails, looking for a pass from F1 (figure 3.16). The options available for F1 are to pass to F3, to shoot and create a rebound for F3, or to pass back to F2 for a shot from the high slot. The key read for F1 is whether the opposing defenseman goes with F3 on the wide drive. This will give an indication of what is open.

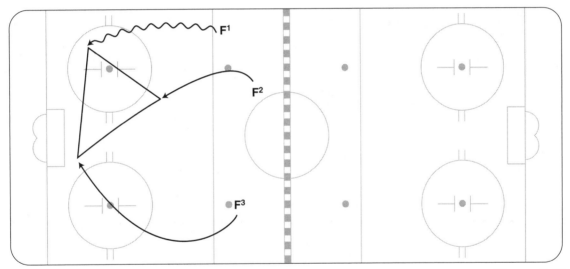

Figure 3.16

■ THREE-ON-TWO MIDLANE DRIVE

A three-on-two entry with a midlane drive gives the puck carrier even more options. Before entering the offensive zone, players should get the puck to the outside of the ice (figure 3.17). Because the two defenders must respect the outmanned situation they find themselves in, their tendency is to back off and allow the entry. Once the puck is to one side or the other, the middle attacking player drives hard toward the net. F2 drives through the mid-ice seam on the inside shoulder of D2. This is the moment defenders get confused and make mistakes. Because the middle player (F2) is seen as attacking the net and has position to do so, D2 has to vacate the prime scoring area. The middle drive completely neutralizes that defender's ability to get involved in what now has turned into a two on one. The far-side winger (F3) moves into the middle-ice shooting area closer to the player with the puck. F1 now has the option of driving and shooting, with F2 going to the net; passing through to F2 for a tip or chance to shoot; or passing to F3 for a high slot shot. This attack allows the potential shot to come from the perfect scoring area and also forces the goaltender to look through the screen provided by F2.

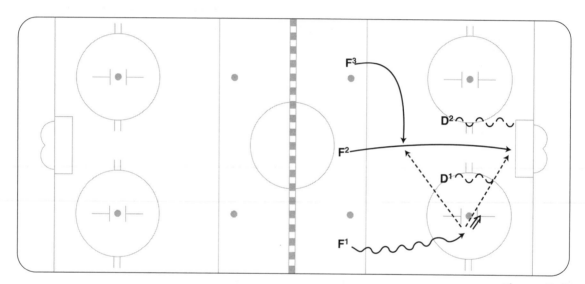

Figure 3.17

■ THREE-ON-TWO TRIPLE DRIVE

In a variation of the midlane drive three on two, all three players initially drive deep (figure 3.18). The puck carrier (F1) takes the puck wide with lots of speed. The middle-ice attacker (F2) continues to drive to the net. This time instead of posting up, F3 attacks the net. The player with the puck (F1) presses hard toward the net, driving outside the near defender, and then immediately cuts hard inside. This creates separation and a chance to make a variety of plays or take a shot against the grain from the prime scoring area. It is important that F2 and F3 drive hard to allow F1 more space to work with. If F1 is skating down his off side (left-hand shot skating down the right wing), he will be in a better position to shoot and make a play because he will have the puck on the forehand.

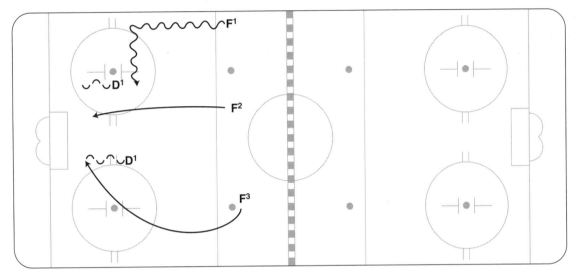

Figure 3.18

■ THREE-ON-TWO DRIVE AND DELAY

In the world of hockey, as in most sports, speed kills. Outside offensive zone speed has a tendency to back off defenders, and this is where our next offensive zone entry tactic works wonders. The player driving outside with the puck looks as if he will drive the puck hard toward the net, but then just at the right moment, this player pivots or tight turns (always to the outside or away from the defender) and skates back toward the blue line (figure 3.19). This delay creates what every hockey player wants: time and space to make the next move. Initially, the defender will have to give space because he is afraid of the deep drive, and as a result it will take a second or two to react to the delay.

A couple of teaching keys allow this excellent offensive tactic to work. The outside-drive player (F1) must "sell" the drive to the net. The perfect time to turn up is when the offensive player is level with or forcing the defender to pivot toward the offensive player. Today's high-speed, high-pace game gives players with the puck very little time to make good plays. This is where creating offensive gaps between the player with the puck and the defenders is critical. Wayne Gretzky, an amazing player, scored a very high percentage of his goals off this tactic of driving, pivoting, gaining middle ice, and shooting.

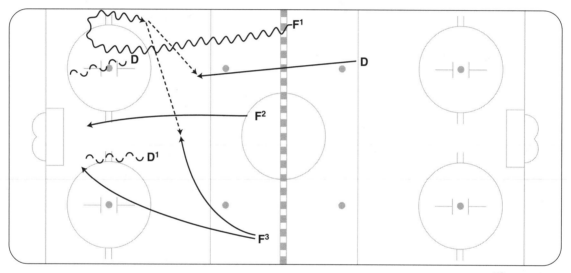

Figure 3.19

■ PRESS-AND-PULL PLAY

A wrinkle in this outside-drive play is being executed often at the NHL level. As the middle-drive offensive player (F2) drives toward the net, he doesn't stay in front of the net but pulls away and finds a shooting "soft spot" (not in the middle of the slot) toward the side of the net where the player with the puck (F1) is turning (figure 3.20). As F1 turns back up-ice he makes a quick inside pass to F2.

   This is a very effective play off the rush because it drives the defender to the net and then creates separation from this defender, who is reluctant to leave the front of the net. Rush plays like the press and pull are effective because of their drive north and then pull south effect. This play obviously creates better shots (sometimes one-timers) as the drive-and-pull offensive player pulls off on his shooting side (it is much tougher to have impact off the backhand).

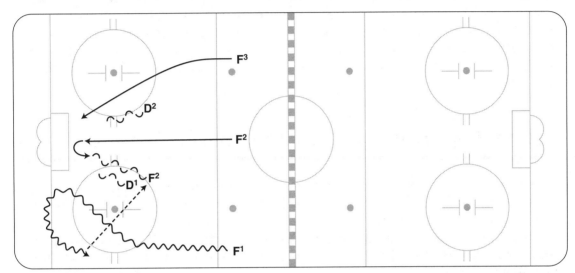

Figure 3.20

Offsides

Entry into the offensive zone can create one of a coach's many pet peeves, the offside. High-level coaches speak often about controlling the controllables. John Wooden, the great basketball coach, said, "I don't worry too much about winning and losing. I worry a lot about practicing the details that deliver the win." One of the details that deliver the win is to never, never, never put yourself or your team offside. Offsides come from selfish possession of the puck or lazy actions where the puck carrier in each case waits too long to make a play and his teammates go offside while trying to anticipate a pass. Yes, opponents can have a positional influence on the offside, but more often than not the offside is created by the team with the puck instead of the team without the puck. Coaches keep count of offsides by play and by line. Puck possession is so hard to get and so hard to keep, why would a team easily give up a puck that they fought so hard to retrieve?

Activating Defense Into Offensive Zone Entries

After a successful breakout or regroup, with the puck in possession of the forwards, one defenseman should follow up as a late-wave option or as one of the three attacking players. As mentioned in the breakout chapter sometimes the center gets caught low in coverage, so it is important to have one defenseman in the rush. When a defenseman moves up to join the rush, he should read the quality of puck possession. Does your teammate have the puck under control while advancing up the ice? If so, then one defenseman must be activated into the rush. Is it risky to have an active defense? Well, the answer is no. The responsibility is in the hands of the puck carrier; he must make good decisions and pick the right options. A defenseman should join and stay in the rush from the breakout, through the neutral zone, and then read the quality of puck possession at the offensive blue line.

By joining the rush and staying in as the third or fourth attacker, the defenseman creates confusion as opponents try to figure out their coverage on the backcheck. Plus an active defenseman usually results in more odd-man rushes because he can get up the ice quicker than the other team backchecks. If the quality of puck possession is good, defensemen should have the green light to go to the net, but make sure they know that they cannot stop and "hang out" in front for the puck—they have to get back to the blue line. Allowing your defense to join the rush is a good strategy, but you don't want it to cost you the other way and give the opposition a chance to get an odd-man rush.

Chapter 4
Attack Zone

Cycling. Setting up behind the net. Activating the defense in the offensive zone. Exploiting the high seam area. Protecting the puck low to buy time and find players who are open. Getting open off the puck. Screening the goaltenders. Making tight plays to sticks at the net. These are all tactics and strategies in the attacking zone.

Once an attacking team has possession in the offensive zone, the brilliant coaches in the great game of hockey really turn on the creative juices. The goal of every attacking team is to create offensive chances. What constitutes a "chance" differs from coach to coach, but in essence, a chance is a shot taken from inside the scoring area. There are three general philosophies to create these offensive chances:

1. Shooting through traffic
2. Creating separation
3. Creating deception

Taking shots through traffic (players in front of the goaltender) will obviously distract the goaltender or deny him the opportunity to see the puck. Goalies are so good these days that a shot without traffic between the shooter and the goalie in many instances is a giveaway. All of the top offensive teams make sure that one player is always in the net area and moving across the sight lines of the goaltender or planted in front of the goaltender. Often this tactic results in the opposition trying to clear the net by moving this player which results in a double screen or possibly a penalty. Both favor the offensive team.

In the separation tactic, the puck carrier creates the time and space needed to make successful plays and create shots. Players away from the puck have to work to get open and separate from their check. They should move to areas where they can receive a pass and be ready to one time the puck or shoot quickly. Sometimes players off the puck can move into an area and then push off their check or push back into an open space. It sounds like a simple principle to separate from your check but I find that a lot of offensive players off the puck skate into their check and essentially "check themselves". When you watch smart players they always seem to be able to get open and as a result they always have the puck.

The puck carrier also needs to be deceptive so that the defending team doesn't know whether he is going to shoot or pass. Deception tactics include faking a shot or pass or simply looking the defender off. Looking the defender off the puck means looking at an option, making a motion to pass in that direction and then skating or moving in another direction. Usually the defender will turn his feet toward the first look and as a result give the offensive player room to move by. Coaches often talk about the triple threat position and we mention it several times in this book. When an offensive player has the puck he should always keep it by the hip on his forehand side which gives him the option of passing, shooting, or making a move on the defender. This triple threat position creates deception simply by where the puck is and the options available. All of these tactics play themselves out through many practiced and set plays that we will now explore.

Cycling

Many offensive strategies include cycling the puck. Younger, inexperienced players often get the cycling process wrong, so let's start with this basic tactic. The cycle works best when the player with the puck deep in the offensive zone begins to bring the puck up the boards toward the blue line (figure 4.1). Generally a defender will press this puck carrier toward the boards and work to remove the puck. The key to the cycle setup is the second offensive forward. This forward mirrors the positioning of the puck carrier but stays 10 or 15 feet (3.0 to 4.6 m) away from the puck carrier on the boards, toward the goal line. This player calls for the puck. Here is where inexperienced players mess up. The tendency is for players to pass into open ice, but the cycle doesn't work best this way. It works best when the puck is angled off the boards, away from the defender's stick, so it bounces off the boards and onto the stick of the second offensive forward. Cycling is an effective tactic when executed correctly.

The purpose of the cycle is to keep possession of the puck and take it to the net to create a scoring chance. If the initial player with the puck can gain a lane to the net, he shouldn't cycle—he should take the puck to the net. A pet peeve of many coaches is when players cycle for the sake of cycling and don't read when to exploit the defenders. If the puck carrier feels pressure and knows the lane is shut down, he should lay the puck back to the corner where he came from. His support player (F2) needs to read this and move to support the cycle pass. Once this play is made, F2 may continue the cycle with a pass back to F3.

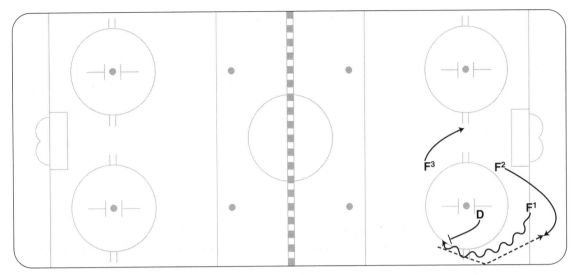

Figure 4.1   Cycling.

The three forwards should move in sequence from the boards to the slot to the net and back to the corner to support the cycle . . . thus the name. The goal of the cycle is to pull a defender out of position and then attack the net or the seams with a quick pass to the open player. Opponents often get their coverage confused because of the quick rotation of players who cycle with the puck then lay it to the corner and work to get open. The cycle is not easy to continuously defend, and when defending the cycle a missed assignment means an offensive chance. The cycle works best along the side boards but can also be used near the back of the net.

The net cycle (figure 4.2) is another cycling option. If well executed, it pulls defenders from the front of the net toward the corner or behind the net, and this movement often opens up passing lanes for excellent scoring chances. It is similar to the side board cycle where one player skates behind the net with the puck and when pressured passes the puck back behind the net. Also it forces the goaltender to follow the play behind the net while trying to keep track of options in front, which is difficult.

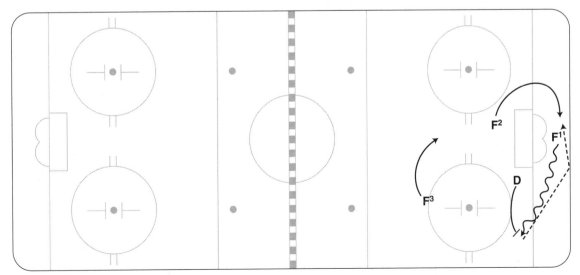

Figure 4.2   The net cycle.

It is important off any cycle play to get the puck to the net quickly. Whether the cycle is on the side boards or behind the net, as soon as the first cycle pass is made that player should look to take the puck to the net or shoot the puck at the net right away. Quick plays like this catch the defensive team off guard and also catch the goaltender trying to adjust. In most situations when a quick shot is taken it will result in a rebound because the goaltender is not set. The other players going to the net should do so with their stick on the ice ready to play the rebound or for a potential shot pass play.

Playing Behind the Net

Wayne Gretzky played behind the net so well, that this area became known as his "office." Gaining offensive positioning behind the net opens up many opportunities for direct-shot (high-percentage) chances. To effectively use the back of the net teams should automatically move the puck to this space when they don't have another option. The offensive player at the net now reads his teammate is in trouble and moves to the back of the net area. When a pass is made to the back of the net the offensive team will always get there first because the defensive team never overplays this area. Using the back of the net forces the opposing defense and goaltender to focus on that area while losing track of where players are in front. Sometimes two defenders can be drawn into this area; if the defensemen are unsure of who should be covering the player behind the net, both may jump in at the same time. Now at least one offensive player will be open in the dangerous scoring area in front of the net.

One of the most effective plays from behind the net occurs when an offensive defenseman skates hard from the point (blue line) looking to receive a pass in the slot (figure 4.3). If the defenseman pressing the net is unable

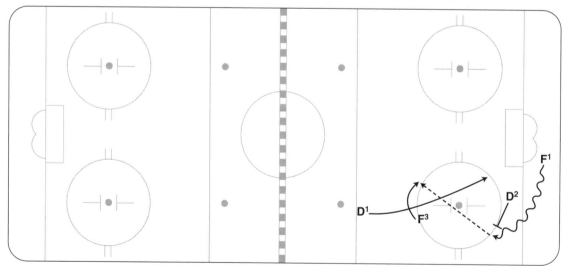

Figure 4.3   Pressing the net.

to receive a clear pass, the second option off of this play becomes very dangerous. As this defenseman moves to the front of the net—pulling as many defenders with him as possible—the boards-side forward steps into this "soft spot" vacuum and often gets to take a dangerous shot through the traffic created by the pressing defenseman.

The second play selection from behind the net (figure 4.4) is also hard to defend. The big decision that defenders must make about the offensive player standing behind the net with the puck is when or how they should flush him out from behind the net. If the defending defenseman attacks the offensive player from one side of the net, two options open up.. The first is that players in high-percentage scoring areas may be left open. The second option is for the player with the puck to reverse the flow and create some "back-door" deception. When flushed out, the player with the puck angles the puck (similar the half-boards cycle) to a teammate filling this flushed-out position. Defenders who were focused on the player being flushed out must now divert their attention back toward the other side of the net. This refocus often opens up back-door or back-side plays.

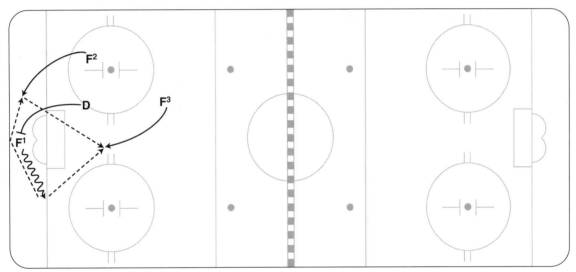

Figure 4.4 Options for a player being flushed from behind the net.

Stretching the Zone: Low–High Plays

With many teams playing a collapsing defensive style (one where all five defenders play low in the offensive zone), it is often difficult in the attacking zone to penetrate the net area without using low–high plays. Low–high plays spread out the defense and create opportunities to get the puck to scoring areas with more time and space. This strategy must be identified before a game as part of the game plan.

Offensive players with the puck make a quick pass to the point (F1 to D1) when they get the puck low or possibly recover a loose rebound in the corner (figure 4.5). D1 can now make a decision to shoot, move the puck to D2, or pass back to one of the forwards. Having the puck move from down low to the blue line creates a gap in the defensive alignment because the defensive wingers try to rush to their point coverage, leaving space between them and their defense. When all five defensive players are down low, the scoring area is crowded; getting the defensive wingers to move out high creates more space in the slot. Each time defenders scramble to defend the high blue line area, there is opportunity for offensive players to find more time and space to create better offensive chances low. Also, the shot from the point, through traffic, is still a primary option to create scoring chances.

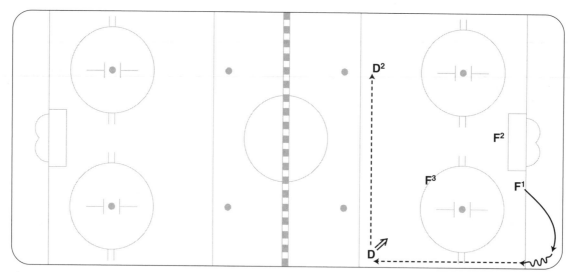

Figure 4.5   Stretching the zone.

Activating Defense in the Offensive Zone

Much like other aspects of offensive play, coaches have to decide how comfortable they are with getting their Ds involved in the offense. Basically, how much risk do they want to take? If the offensive team has quality puck possession, there is little risk in allowing the defense to move in offensively. You have to teach your players to make good decisions with the puck and trust that they will make a safe play rather than a dangerous play. The key rules for defensemen that will help minimize risk are as follows:

1. Only one D at a time goes deep into the offensive zone.

2. Read the time of the game and the score—Ds should be more cautious when moving in offensively late in periods or when your team has the lead.

3. The forwards *must* have quality puck possession in order for the defense to activate.

4. When the defense move in, if a pass is not made do not "hang out"—get back to the blue line quickly.

Attack Zone Plays

This section describes special plays made in the offensive zone using an active defense. The plays are all effective and provide a variety of options.

■ STRONG-SIDE SLIDE

D1 reads that F1 is cycling out of the corner, so he slides down the boards and receives an exchange pass from F1. The exchange is like a handoff in football, where the puck carrier protects the puck and gives it to D1. D1 now has the option of driving the net with the puck or cutting behind the net with possession and looking for a passing option (figure 4.6). F1 should cycle out high and remain in a defensive position until D1 recovers.

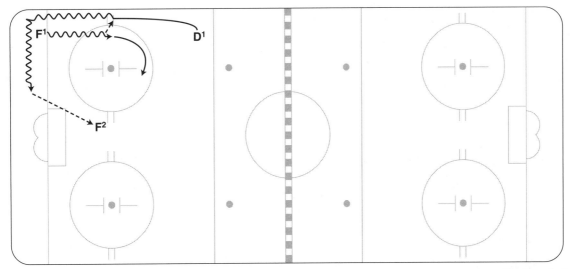

Figure 4.6

■ MIDSEAM PENETRATION

When D1 sees the defensive team overplaying the boards, he should slide into mid-ice and down through the slot toward the net. F1 should use deception by looking as if he will pass to the point and then making a quick pass to D1, who is moving through the middle of the slot. D1 may have an opportunity to shoot quickly or move in deeper (figure 4.7). Once again F1 should move out to a higher defensive position after the pass in case of a turnover.

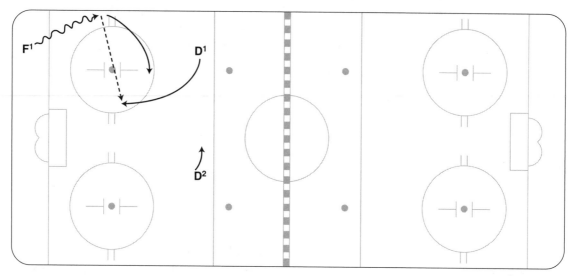

Figure 4.7

■ BACK-SIDE SLIDE

When the offensive player (F1) has the puck and D2 reads that the defensive team is overplaying one side of the ice, D2 should quickly move down the back side and be ready for the pass. F1 tries to find an open seam to thread the pass through to the wide side. If D2 doesn't get the pass when moving in, he should get out immediately. Once again, this play should be made quickly and with deception so that attention is not drawn to the defenseman moving in. This is a riskier play because of the distance of the pass and the number of players in the area but if D2 gets the pass clean he will have a great scoring chance (figure 4.8).

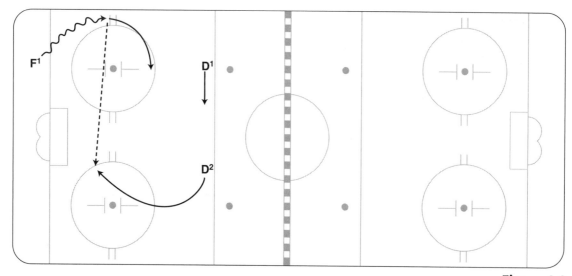

Figure 4.8

Chapter 5
Power Plays

When developing the power play, the coach must go through several steps including selecting a formation, describing the skills necessary for each position, slotting players into positions, developing drills to practice the skills, and finally allowing players to offer input as they mature and possibly the opportunity to select their own options within the framework. Most coaches go through these steps before the season starts once they know the makeup of the team. It is important as a coach to follow these steps, and then review them from time to time as your lineup changes or when you are looking for improvements.

1. **Select a formation.** We will discuss three formations in this chapter. Identify which formation is suited for the abilities of the players available to you. Certain players are more suited to execute one better than another. The differentiating factor is usually the skill level and how good they are at passing, seeing the ice, and shooting off the pass.

2. **Describe skills necessary for each position.** Make a list of all the skills needed to play each position in the formation selected. Keep this as a checklist when working on the power play in practice. Also use it to decide which players in your lineup are best suited to play each position. For example, the following six skills are critical for defensemen on the power play: deception, walking the blue line on the forehand and backhand, shooting, one-timing the puck, seeing the opening and making a pass through the box, and skating into the open seam at the right time. Under the section on zone set up you will find the skills listed for each player. This should help you build a checklist and decide which players are best suited for a particular position.

3. **Slot players into the positions.** Decide based on the skills required where each player should play in the system. On the power play there

will be some interchange, but generally each player will become proficient in one of the five positions. One of the harder positions to play is the front of the net. You would like someone with size who also has very good hands to corral a rebound or quickly release a shot off the pass. This player cannot be afraid of being hit with the puck and needs to have a touch for deflecting and redirecting pucks.

4. **Develop or select drills to practice skills.** Develop a bank of drills to work on the skills of the chosen power-play alignment and also the breakout options. Sometimes the power-play breakout drills can be included with regular breakout practice. When developing in-zone skills, it is definitely better to start with no resistance and then progress to working against penalty killers. Players of all ages need to focus for the first month or so on constant repetitions with no resistance and get their puck movement and timing down before progressing to resistance. If penalty killers are introduced too early in practice situations, it will only lead to frustration.

5. **Allow players freedom to choose the right options.** Much like a quarterback in football, one or two players on the power play should take the lead and pick the best available play or shot. As you will see in the specific alignments, there are five or six set plays to choose from. It is better to have set options than to allow the power play to freelance. Once the players become familiar with the alignments and have practiced them enough, the options will become instinctive. Let the power play group watch video on a regular basis so they become familiar with the options that arise with different penalty-kill alignments and pressure.

6. **Repeat for specific situations.** All of the previous steps must now be repeated for five-on-three and four-on-three situations.

When developing and monitoring the power play, coaches should remember that small details create the power. These are the little things that make a successful power play.

○ **Outwork the penalty-killing unit.** Recognizing that they have the advantage, most power plays let up a bit with regard to effort, but this shouldn't happen.

○ **Give your team momentum** by getting scoring chances and shots. At all levels the best power plays units only score on 2 out of every 10 power plays, but you should create momentum for your team on every power play.

○ **Look confident**—never show dejection or defeat. Body language is so important in sports. Don't give your opponent any signs that you don't think you can score. Leave the ice with the attitude that you didn't score this time, but it will definitely happen next time.

○ **Have two units with two looks.** Confuse the other team's penalty-killing units by having a different setup for each of your units.

○ **Win the draw!** Face-offs are so key on special teams. It takes 15 to 20 seconds to get set up again in the zone if the other team clears the puck.

○ **Try to give other players on your team an opportunity to go on the power play**—this will do wonders for their confidence. Make sure in practice that all players work on power-play skills.

Power-Play Breakouts

Discussed here are five breakout options and two neutral zone regroup options. All breakouts are diagrammed with D1 starting behind the net, but at times D1 will pick up the puck and look to skate or advance it quickly. This will depend on the penalty-kill pressure and forecheck alignment. Anytime there is no up ice pressure or the penalty killers are changing this is a cue for D1 to turn up ice quickly. In other situations start from behind the net and come up as a coordinated unit. To execute the plays perfectly and efficiently, teams should have only one breakout for each unit or use the same breakout for both.

■ SINGLE SWING

D1 gets the puck behind the net (figure 5.1). D2 swings in one corner, and F1 swings in the other. F2 waits at the near blue line, F3 at the far blue line. As D1 begins to advance up the ice, F2 and F3 start to move across the ice, with both players looking to get open early. Options for D1 are to pass to F1 with support from F2, pass to D2 with support from F3, pass to F2 or F3 early (may use a long bank pass to F3), or skate the puck and rim it to either side.

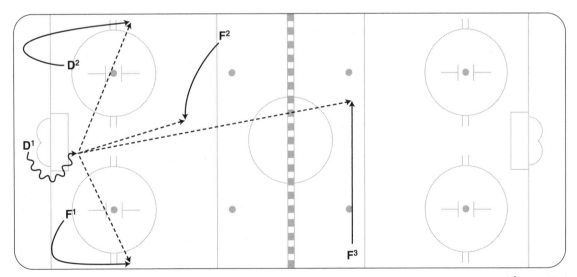

Figure 5.1

■ DALLAS CUT

D1 stops behind the net with the puck (figure 5.2). D2 swings in one corner. F1 and F2 swing in the other, with F1 slightly ahead. F3 stretches. The primary option and one that sometimes can result in a breakaway is for D1 to pass to F2 on the inside angle, trying to split the seam between the defenders. The reason this pass is so effective is that by D1 faking a pass to F1 wide and then passing quickly to F2 on the inside it freezes opposition defense and allows F2 to split the seam with speed. D1 also has the option of passing to F1 who carries the puck in with support from F2; pass to D2, who gets support from F3; pass to F3 early if uncovered; or rim the puck to F1 or F2.

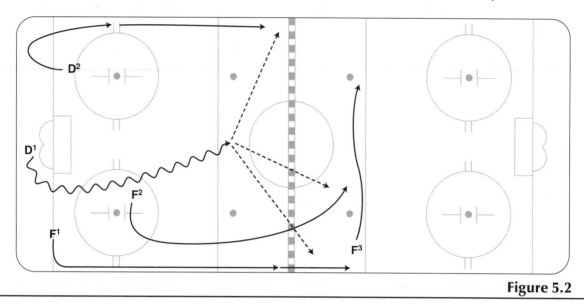

Figure 5.2

■ CANUCK CENTER-LANE OPTION

D1 starts with the puck (figure 5.3). F1 and D2 swing to opposite sides. F2 swings slightly higher on the same side as F1 and looks to get the puck in the middle of the ice. F2 carries the puck through the middle and uses F1 or D2 for support. F3 clears a lane for F2 by stretching across the far blue line. F2 tries to enter the zone with possession and then lay the puck to the outside once defenders are drawn to him.

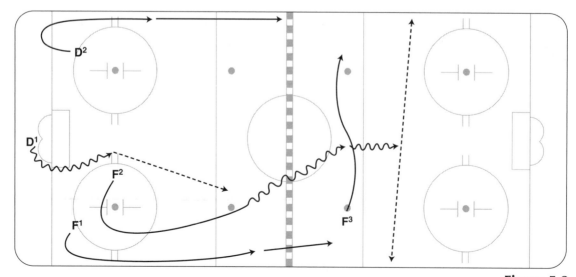

Figure 5.3

■ FIVE BACK

All players come back to the puck. Once the last player is back, all five players start to advance up ice together (figure 5.4). F2 and F3 take the inside lanes while F1 and D2 move up ice along the boards. D1 has the option to pass to the inside players (F2 and F3) or to the outside lanes (F1 and D2). D1 tries to draw the PK'ers into the middle and then dish the puck to speed wide. If D1 skates the puck to center, he can continue into the zone or rim the puck to either side.

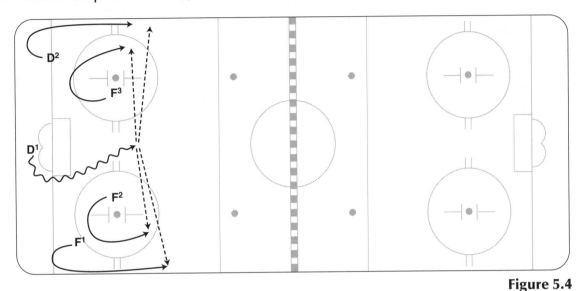

Figure 5.4

■ DROP PASS

The key here is for the late forward to delay long enough to be an option once the defense carries the puck up over the blueline. D1 starts by skating up the middle with F2 and D2 moving up the outside (figure 5.5). F3 stretches and F1 comes late from deep in the zone behind the play. When D1 crosses the blue line he should try to drag the first penalty killer to one side and then lay the puck over to the area where F1 is skating into. The penalty killers who have been backing up with the initial rush now have to slow down and adjust to F1. F1 has too much speed and should be able to weave his way into the zone. F2, F3, and D2 have to be careful not to go offside.

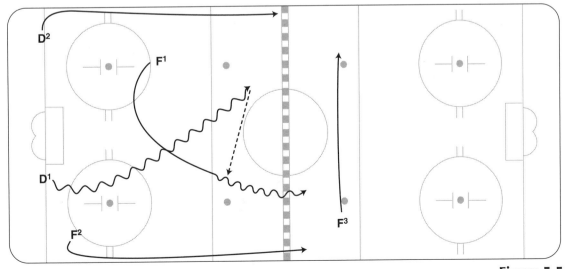

Figure 5.5

There are times on the power play when the offensive team doesn't have to go all the way back and break out from their own end. If the puck is in the neutral zone or just inside the blue line, it is often a waste of time to go all the way back behind the net. Have a plan to break out using half of the ice in a neutral zone counter. The following two plays are great options in this situation.

■ WINGER CROSS

In this option, D1 picks up the puck. F1 and F2 swing to opposite sides and build up speed (figure 5.6). F3 stretches and D2 supports D1. D1 has the option to pass to F2 or F1 with speed on the outside; pass to F3, who may enter the zone or redirect the puck to F1 or F2; or skate the puck and rim it to F1 or F2.

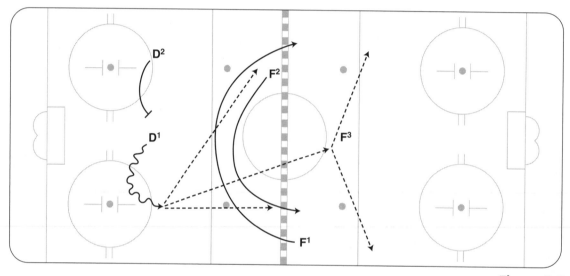

Figure 5.6

■ UP THE GUT

In this option, D2 takes the puck up the ice in a wide lane hoping to draw a defender outside (figure 5.7). As D2 advances, he looks to pass inside to F1, who comes from behind the play and moves with speed through the middle of the ice. F2 and F3 stretch. When the first penalty killer is drawn outside, the middle opens up for F1 to skate into. The second option is to use F2 or F3 on the stretch.

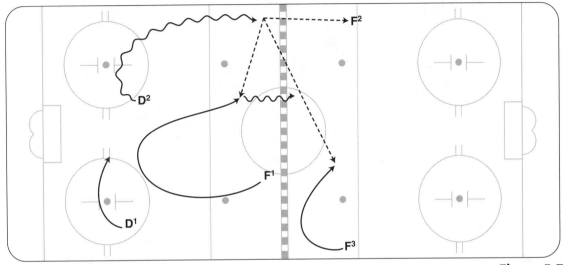

Figure 5.7

Gaining and Maintaining Possession off the Entry

When explaining breakout options to your team, it is important to discuss how the players set up once they are in the offensive zone. Where do they move the puck to get into the formations they have practiced? Many penalty-killing units focus on denying the setup and prepare different tactics to regain possession of the puck once the power play unit is in the zone. Listed here are three ways to ensure that the players are able to set up after a dump-in or clean entry.

1. **Reversing the puck.** When under pressure as he enters the zone, F1 stops or delays and then reverses the puck back up the boards where he came from. This is successful against teams whose strong-side forward comes down low on the entry (figure 5.8). D1 must get up to the offensive blue line quickly to be ready for this play.

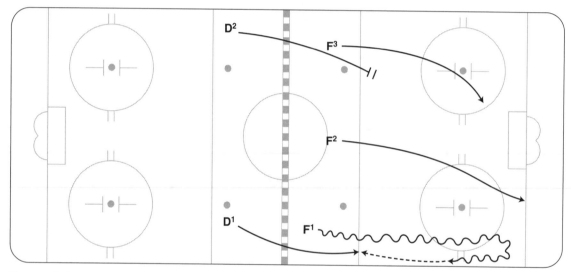

Figure 5.8   Reversing the puck on entry.

2. **Switching sides.** As F1 enters the zone, he sees that all four penalty killers are on one side of the ice, so he immediately passes across the ice to F3. F1 will have to thread the puck through traffic, but it may be the only option to get immediate uncontested possession (figure 5.9).

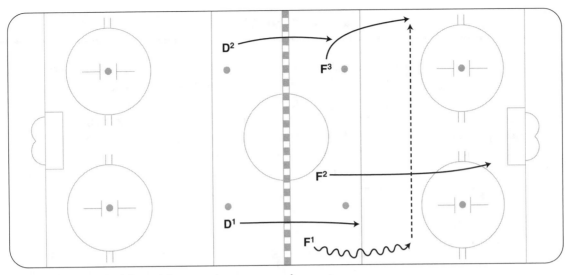

Figure 5.9 Switching sides on the power-play entry.

3. **Recovering the dump-in.** The key to recovering the dump-in is to get all three forwards quickly to the puck. Once the puck is stopped and the forwards are in a battle for possession, F1, F2, or F3 should rim or bank the puck back to the blue line as soon as they get it on their stick. The defensemen should be ready at the corners of the blue line and expect the quick rim pass. The penalty-killing team will probably have three players in the corner for the battle, so this will give the power play time to set up (figure 5.10).

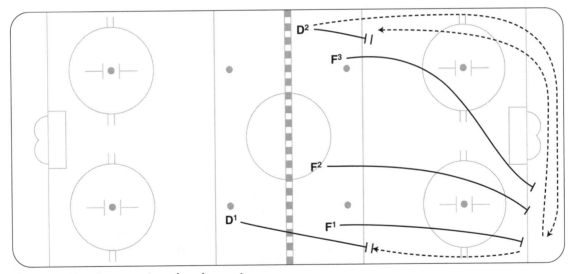

Figure 5.10 Recovering the dump-in.

Zone Setup

Once the players gain possession, they can set up in the zone and use one of the following formations. This section discusses the options for three different power-play formations: the overload, 1-3-1, and split power play. Within each are the descriptions of the various plays and responsibilities of each player. As mentioned earlier, coaches can pick which option suits their players and team. During the season you may change to another setup, but it does take a while to learn all the options and execute properly. Give the players time to get it right.

Overload Power Play

When using the overload power play, either side can be the strong side, with left-hand shots quarterbacking from the half boards on the right side and right shots on the left side. This gives the player a shooting and passing advantage from that area. As the name implies, the setup is overloaded to the strong side, with four players on that half of the ice. In this setup, much like most power-play setups, net presence is critical for success. It is important that the net player be in a screen position most of the time but also available to pop out into a scoring area. When setting up the overload and moving the puck, the team should try to twist the box around by having the strong-side D move quickly across the blue line and even go beyond the halfway point before passing back to the half boards or over to D2.

Half-Boards Player

The half-boards player is the key quarterback of this setup, with D1 playing a secondary role. The half-boards player must slide up and down the boards, distribute the puck, and shoot from the outside, all while under pressure. He has to be calm and poised with the puck and quick to recognize where to move the puck. Penalty killers will either force the half-boards player with their D from down low or their forward from the top, so this player must be able to move with the pressure, protect the puck, and make a play.

Strong-Side Point Man

The strong-side defenseman is the other key player in this overload setup. He along with the half-boards player will have the puck the most and be the ones to settle the play down and set up. Keep your feet on the blue line to create space between yourself and the penalty killers. This extra room will give you time to make decisions or step into a shot, while drawing out the penalty killers and creating seams in behind. This player needs to have a shooting mentality and always be a threat to shoot. The number one way to score and create chances on the power play is still to take a point shot with net traffic. Sometimes the shot can be a wrist shot, and other times the D should shoot hard. The penalty killers shouldn't know whether the D is going to shoot or pass—have good deception. When pressured, move the puck to the half-boards player or the back-side D, or make a quick, low play.

Low Walk Player

The low walk player should have his feet on the goal line and stay close to the net in order to attack quickly and also move in to screen the goaltender or get a rebound. If this player drifts too far to the outside, he cannot do either. The low walk player must be versatile and quick. At times he will switch with the half-boards player, usually when there is no option available as the half-boards player drives the net. This tactic forces the penalty killers to adjust quickly and often creates passing options. Before the game, find out how the other team forces—will they pressure quickly with the low defenseman, or will they hold the front of the net? This information will help determine what option might be available and where the pressure will come from.

Net Man

The net player's main job is to screen the goaltender on all shots and then be ready to play rebounds. Although it sounds simple, it requires courage to stand in front of shots and a lot of skill to deflect them. When the puck is moved low, the net player should slide out to the low slot or back door (on the back post away from coverage) to wait for a pass. Either option is good, but it should be predetermined before the game so the low player knows where to pass the puck. Sometimes the net player is so anxious to get available for a low play that he loses the screen position when players above him are ready to shoot. The screen is very important because you want the opposing goaltender to have to work to see the puck. Make the goaltender's job tough.

Sliding Back-Side D

The back-side defenseman initially provides a release to get the puck away from pressure and also supports the strong-side D when he is under pressure. He will be a threat to score because he is outside the vision of the penalty killers. He sometimes gets lost as the penalty killers focus on the overload side. Move up and down the far side of the ice, staying in line with the position of the puck. Go down as far as the goal line and up as high as the blue line. If you recover a loose puck on the far side, set up on the half boards and then briefly work the setup from there.

Zone Options for the Overload Power Play

The following are the options for the overload power play. All need to become automatic in practice in order for them to be executed well in the game. Depending on the skill level of the players involved and also on how the opposing penalty killers force, certain options will be more successful than others. Coaches should prepare the players for the resistance they may face from the penalty killers so they know ahead of time what plays to concentrate on.

■ BACK-SIDE D SLIDE AND SHOOT

Move the puck around to D2, who slides down the back side and looks to shoot and score, shoot for a deflection, or pass across to F1 for a one-timer (figure 5.11). The play back to F1 is a more difficult play to execute because of the skill required to shoot off the pass. F1 should be wide and prepared to receive a pass around the top of the opposite circle.

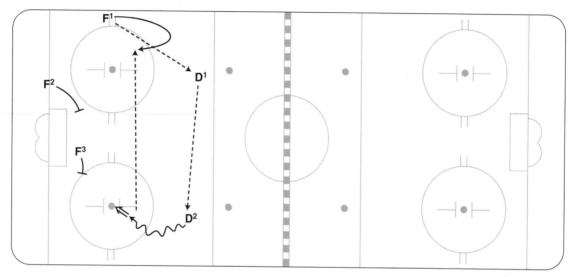

Figure 5.11

■ STRONG-SIDE D SHOT

Move the puck from F2 to F1 to D1. D1 slides across the blue line, looking to take a slapshot or wrist the puck through to the net (figure 5.12). F3 must be in a tight screen position. F2, F1, and D2 must be ready to converge on rebounds. D1 must fake the shot against teams that block and look to get the puck by the screen. Establishing a shot from this area on a consistent basis always results in the most power play chances but D1 must have deception along with a good shot.

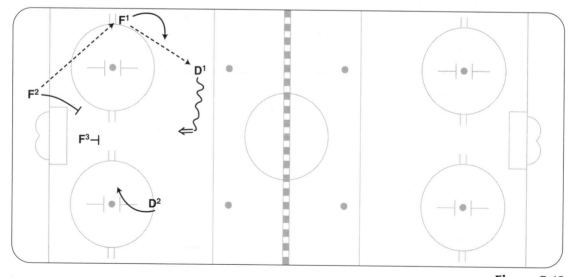

Figure 5.12

■ HALF-BOARDS SHOT

F2 moves the puck up to F1, who passes to D1. D1 walks across the line, drawing a penalty killer with him (figure 5.13). D1 fakes a shot and passes back to F1. F1 should have followed D1 up the half boards, initially staying wide . Once F1 receives the pass he moves off the boards and shoots. F3 screens while F2 and D2 converge for rebounds.

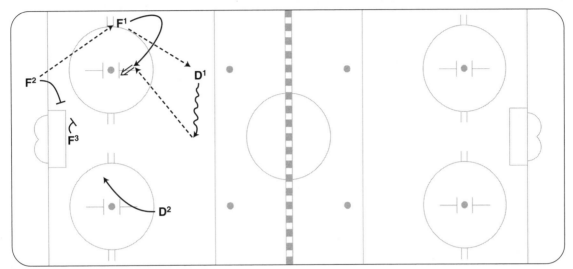

Figure 5.13

■ LOW PLAY OPTION

F2 passes to F1, who passes to D1 (figure 5.14). D1 fakes a shot and passes back to F1, who rolls off the half boards, fakes a shot, and passes to F2. F2 now has the option of taking the puck to the net and shooting, taking the puck to the net and passing to F3 on the back side or to F3 in the slot area. The decision for F3 to be on the backdoor or in the slot depends on how the other team plays this situation. It is best if teams vary where F3 goes so the opponent never knows where he is going to be. D2 should move opposite to F3 and move to the slot or back side. F2 also has the option on this low play to take the puck behind the net and pass out to F3 or back to F1 or D2.

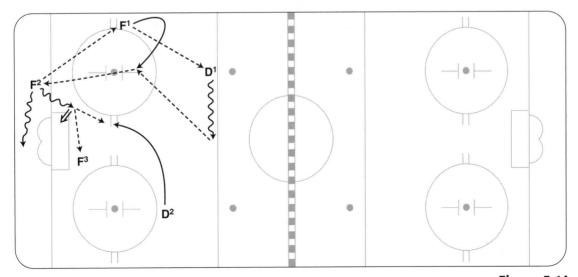

Figure 5.14

■ HALF-BOARDS INTERCHANGE

After the players learn the previous options, it is important to add some interchange so that the penalty killers' job becomes more difficult. Whenever F1 passes the puck to F2 and no immediate play results, they should get in the habit of switching positions. F1 passes to F2 and drives the net, looking to get the puck back (which he may). If there is no play, F2 cycles up the boards and starts to look for new options. F1 replaces F2 low (figure 5.15).

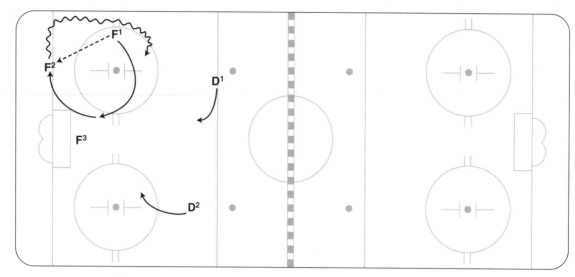

Figure 5.15

■ SLIDING D INTERCHANGE

This is a more complicated maneuver, but it adds a lot of confusion to the penalty killers' alignment. After D1 slides along the blue line and passes back to F1 (figure 5.16), he may move to the net (this should be predetermined). As D1 goes to the net, F3 slides out to the side, and D2 moves up top on the blue line. F1 now makes a quick play as this is happening. F1 may use any of the previous options because the alignment is the same. D1 holds a strong position at the net and remains there until a goal is scored or the puck is cleared.

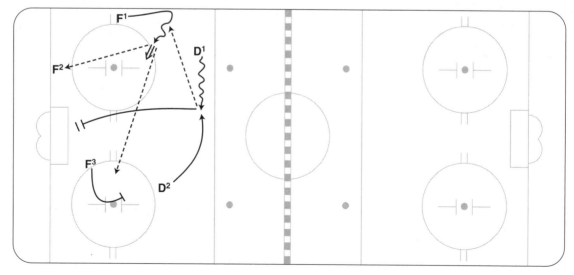

Figure 5.16

1-3-1 Power Play

The 1-3-1 power play is one of the newer power-play formations used by several teams today. Essentially there are two strong sides, with the puck being able to be controlled on either half boards. It is easy to switch sides either up top or behind the net to settle the puck out when under pressure or to create chances. Once again, net presence is critical. The key to success with this formation is for the top three players to focus on shooting or one-timing the puck. This power play is difficult for pressure penalty-killing units to defend because of the side-to-side options.

Right and Left Side Half-Boards Players

Set up with the right shot on the left boards and the left shot on the right. These two players are definitely the quarterbacks. Both must be a threat to shoot or fake the shot and pass while also being calm under pressure. They should work the puck up to the high D as number one option, and don't force plays through the box—often the play through the box will open up after recovering a rebound.

Mid-Ice Point Man

An important strategy for this defenseman is to keep his feet on the blue line to allow more room to make a play or step into a shot. Slide along the line with deception while looking to find an open lane to the net. Quickly work the puck from left to right if the shot isn't there, and then look to shoot again. Wrist shots to the net are also good, but if there is a chance for a slapshot, use it. In the 1-3-1 setup, the puck should revolve around this player.

Slot Player

This can be a defenseman who slides in or a forward who plays defense and then moves into the slot area. Move into this position once the puck is under control. Depending on whether this player is a right or left shot, from one side he must be ready for a quick release shot and from the other side a shot pass. The shot pass is a play where the outside players shoot to the stick of the slot player for a redirect on the net. The slot player should move around in the space to distract the penalty killers. It is key that this player is ready to support both half-boards players when they are in trouble.

Net Man

The net man, as the name indicates, plays the net area unless support is needed to settle the puck out. He may release to the strong side for a low pass and the potential to make a quick inside play. This is a good strategy, but the player has to read whether the high players are shooting or whether they need a low option. Stay active, and get into shooting lanes at the right time.

Zone Options for the 1-3-1 Power Play

The following are four options for the 1-3-1 power play. As with the overload power play, all need to become automatic in practice in order to be executed well in the game. Depending on the skill level of the players involved and also on how the opposing penalty killers force, certain options will be more successful than others. Coaches should prepare the players for the resistance they may face from the penalty killers so they know ahead of time what plays to concentrate on. Note that all options may be run from either side.

■ POINT SHOT

F1 passes to D1. D1 passes to F2, who passes back to D1 for a shot (figure 5.17). This may be a one-timer depending on what shot the defenseman is. All players should fake a shot before passing. F3 keeps a tight screen. D2, F1, and F2 converge on the rebound.

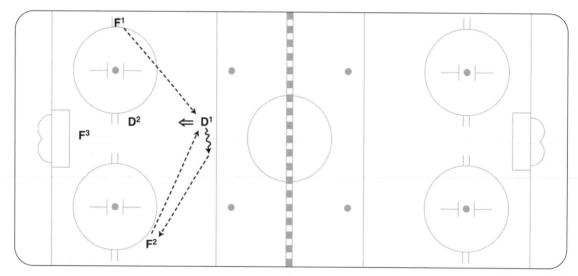

Figure 5.17

■ HALF-BOARDS SHOT OR CROSS-ICE PASS

F1 passes to D1 (figure 5.18). D1 passes to F2, who has the option of shooting or passing to F1. There will be several times during the power play when the cross-ice seam will be available. Remember this is a more difficult option to execute because of the skill level required to thread the pass across ice and one time the puck. Good deception from F2 will create an open lane to F1. F3 keeps a tight screen. D2, F1, and F2 converge on the rebound.

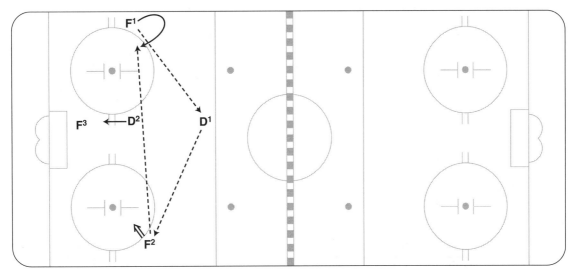

Figure 5.18

■ INSIDE PLAY

F1 passes to D1, who passes to F2 (figure 5.19). F2 fakes the shot and passes inside to D2 for a one-timer or redirect play. This inside play can be made from either side. D2 must be ready for a pass at all times. F3 keeps a tight screen. F1 and F2 converge on the rebound. Depending on which shot D2 is, this may be on opportunity for a quick release shot or shot pass deflection.

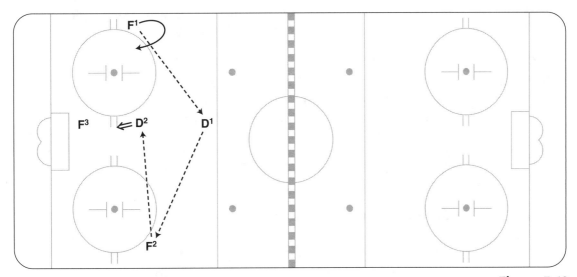

Figure 5.19

■ LOW-RELEASE PLAY

F1 passes to D1 (figure 5.20). D1 passes to F2. F3 releases from the net (in this case he would be a left shot). F2 passes to F3. F3 makes an inside play to D2 or back-side play to F1. F3 could also take the puck to the net. This option is tough to defend against.

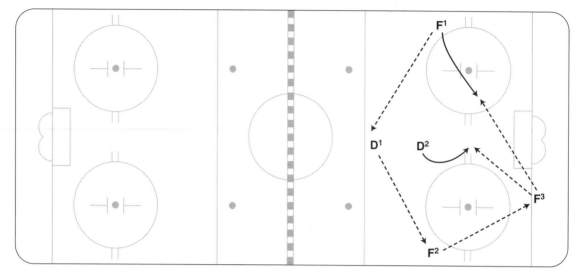

Figure 5.20

Split Power Play

The third power-play option in this section is the split power play. With two strong sides, it has more of a spread look to it, and like the 1-3-1 it is easy to switch sides either up top or behind the net. Once again, net presence is critical. It is important that the two defensemen up top be prepared to shoot. When this happens, they will find that seams will open up for the forwards down low. This power play is also difficult for pressure penalty-killing units because of the side-to-side options. The split power play can easily be twisted into an overload setup and back again.

Two Blue Line Defensemen

The two defensemen on the blue line need to keep their feet on the line to create more space between them and the penalty killers. They should be about dot width apart. Once the puck is moved up top, always quickly relay it from D to D to spread out the penalty killers. Work the puck from left to right while looking to shoot. The defensemen may slide along the line with deception to find an open lane to the net. If there isn't much time or space, wrist shots to the net are also good.

Right and Left Side Half-Boards Players

These players set up and operate in a similar way to the 1-3-1 power play, with the left shot on the right boards and the right shot on the left boards. Both players should be a threat to shoot or fake the shot and pass. Stay calm under pressure. The number one option should be to work the puck up to the high Ds especially when being pressured low. Don't force plays through the box—often the play through the box will open up after recovering a rebound.

Net Man

With most of these power-play setups the net man's job description doesn't change much. This player should stay at the net unless support is needed to settle the puck out but may release to either side for a low pass. Stay active, and get into shooting lanes at the right time. Support the half-boards players when they are in trouble and under pressure by sliding out to the side of the net. To settle the puck out when pressured down low, simply relay the puck behind the net to the opposite half-boards player.

Zone Options for the Split Power Play

The following are the options for the split power play. Practice all options so the players can do them automatically. Then in a game, they will be able to pick the best option depending on how the penalty killers react to the puck movement and shots. Coaches should prepare the team for the resistance they may face from the penalty killers so they know ahead of time what plays to concentrate on. Note that all options may be run from either side.

■ D-TO-D POINT SHOT

F1 passes to D1, who passes to D2 (figure 5.21). D2 slides down a step for a shot. This may be a one-timer depending on what shot the defenseman is. F3 keeps a tight screen on the goaltender. F1 and F2 converge on the rebound. Usually if the shot is low the goaltender will have trouble keeping the rebound from going to one of the side players F1 or F2.

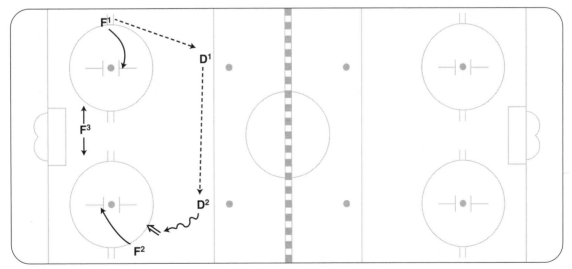

Figure 5.21

■ D-TO-D AND BACK

F1 passes to D1, who passes to D2 (figure 5.22). D2 slides down a step for a fake shot. D2 passes back to D1 in mid-ice for a shot. This may be a one-timer depending on what shot the defenseman is. F3 keeps a tight screen. F1 and F2 converge on the rebound.

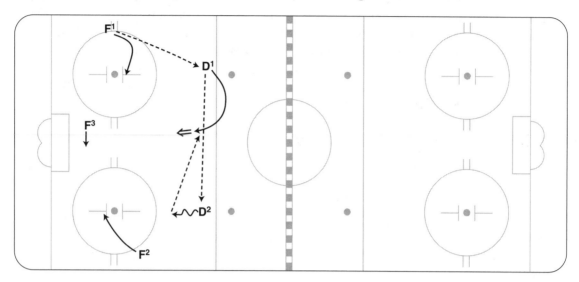

Figure 5.22

■ D-TO-D CROSS-SEAM PASS

F1 passes to D1, who passes to D2 (figure 5.23). D2 slides down a step for a fake shot. D2 passes to F1 for a one-timer or quick-release shot. F3 keeps a tight screen. F2 converges on the rebound.

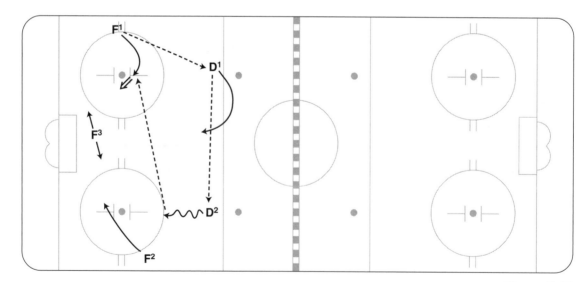

Figure 5.23

DOUBLE-SEAM PASS

F1 passes to D1, who passes to D2 (figure 5.24). D2 slides down a step for a fake shot. D2 passes to F1, who fakes the shot and passes cross-ice to F2 for a one-timer or quick-release shot. F3 keeps a tight screen. F1 converges on the rebound.

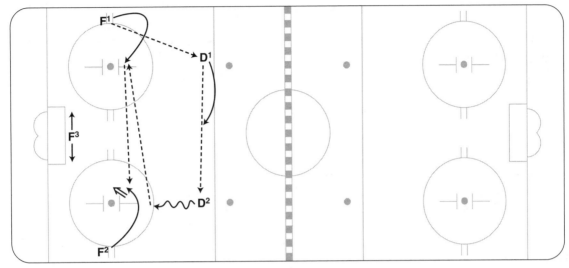

Figure 5.24

LOW-RELEASE PLAY

F1 passes to D1, who passes to D2. D2 slides down a step and passes back to D1 in mid-ice (figure 5.25). D1 fakes a shot and passes to F1. F1 fakes a shot and passes low to F3 at the side of the net. F3 takes the puck to the net or passes to F2 on the back door.

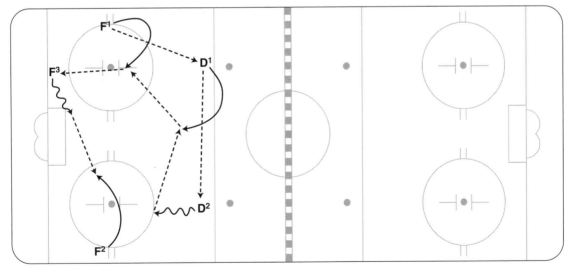

Figure 5.25

Five-on-Three Power Play

The five-on-three opportunity is often a turning point in the game because unlike other power-play opportunities, which operate at a 20 percent success rate, a five on three should result in a goal 50 percent of the time. Most fans expect 100 percent, but the thing to remember with the five on three is that you rarely get a full two minutes. Identified here are three options to use—the goal-line 2-3, the motion 2-3, and the umbrella. Pick the one you like best, and work on it with your team. There are enough plays within each to have variety, but remember you want to score and you may not have a lot of time, so get your players to execute well.

■ GOAL-LINE 2-3

There are a number of options off this 2-3 power-play setup. F1 should be a right shot and F2 a left shot. Some coaches like D1 and D2 to play their regular sides, and others like D1 and D2 to be the same shot. Here are the options with D1 and D2 being left shots: D1 to D2 to F2 and a quick low pass across to F1 (figure 5.26 a, number 1); D1 to D2 to F2 and a pass to F3 in the slot (figure 5.26a, number 2); F1 to D1 to D2 for a one-timer shot (figure 5.26b, number 3); or F1 can pass directly to D2 for a one-timer (figure 5.26b, number 4).

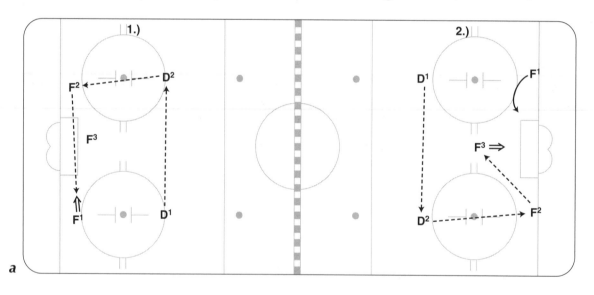

a

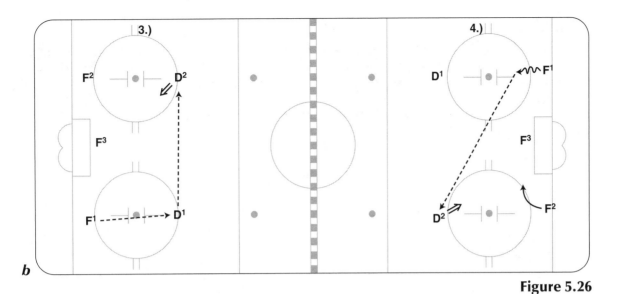

Figure 5.26

◼ MOTION 2-3

This is the same as the previous setup but with motion to create confusion. Penalty killers become so good at staying in lanes that some movement might be needed. D1 and D2 are both left shots in these two options:

1. F1 to D1 to D2. After faking a shot, D2 slides flat across the ice (figure 5.27, left side). D1 moves behind D2. D2 can shoot, pass down to F1 or F2 for a quick shot, or pass back to D1 for a one-timer.

2. F1 to D1 and back to F1 (figure 5.27, right side). D1 skates to the front of the net. D2 slides across, and F2 moves up high. F1 can pass to D2 or F2 for a one-timer, to F3 on the back side, or to D1 sliding in.

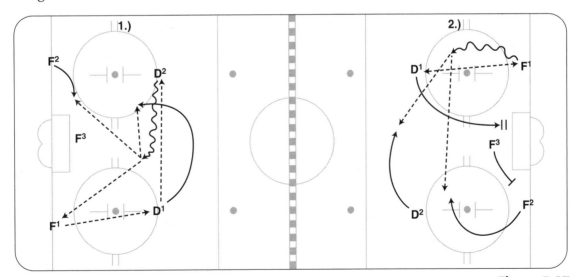

Figure 5.27

■ UMBRELLA

For this example, D1 is a right shot, D2 is a left shot, and F1 is a right shot. Both low players (F2 and F3) slide in and out as a screen and low pass option. Options on the umbrella setup include the following: F1 to D1 to D2 for a one-timer (figure 5.28a, number 1); F1 to D1 to D2 and back to F1 for a one-timer (figure 5.28a, number 2); F1 to D1 to D2 and back to D1 for a one-timer (figure 5.28b, number 3); or F1 to D1 to D2 and then low to F2, who can pass to F3 or back to D1 (figure 5.28b, number 4).

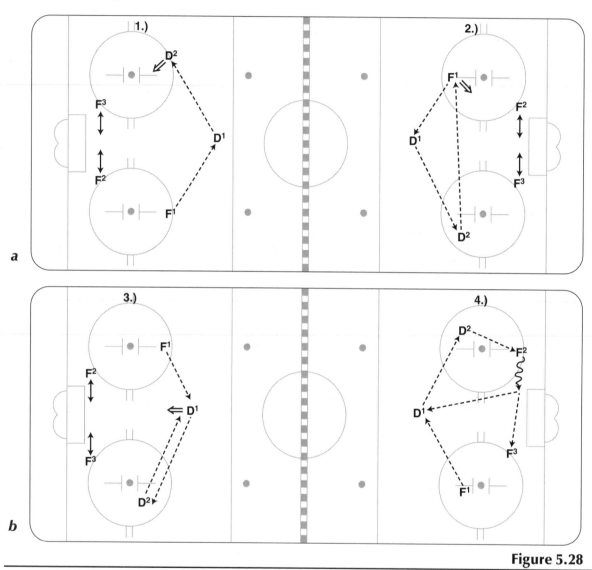

Figure 5.28

Four-on-Three Power Play

The four-on-three power play is the least common of the man-advantage opportunities that occur in a game. There are two basic setups: the box and the umbrella. The umbrella is more suited for teams that have a big one-timer shooter up top; the box is better for teams that can make quick, low plays once the shot from the point is taken away.

■ BOX

When using this setup, you need to make sure one of the low players is in a screen position when D1 or D2 shoots. Both forwards and both Ds should be opposite shots. D1 passes to D2, who passes to F1. F1 passes across to F2 for a quick shot (figure 5.29, number 1). D1 and D2 can also pass the puck back and forth, looking for a one-timer (figure 5.29, number 2). Often the penalty killers will overplay the one-timer shots up top and leave a quick two on one low for the forwards.

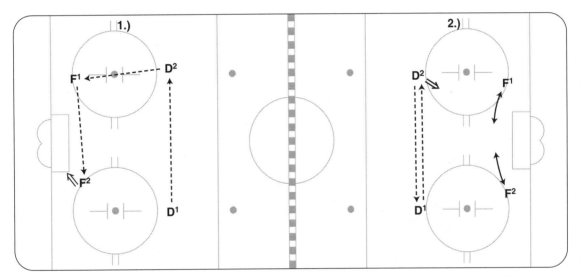

Figure 5.29

■ UMBRELLA

For this example, D1 is a left shot, D2 is a left shot, and F1 is a right shot. F2 screens in front. Options for the umbrella setup are similar to the five-on-three set-up, with D1, D2, and F1 looking to get a quick one-timer shot. They may move around slightly but generally stay in the high triangle setup. Here are the options: F1 to D1 to D2 for a one-timer; F1 to D1 to D2 and back to F1 for a one-timer (figure 5.30a, number 2); F1 to D1 to D2 and back to D1 for a one-timer (figure 5.30b, number 3); or F1 to D1 to D2 and then low to F2, who can pass to D1 or across to F1 (figure 5.30b, number 4).

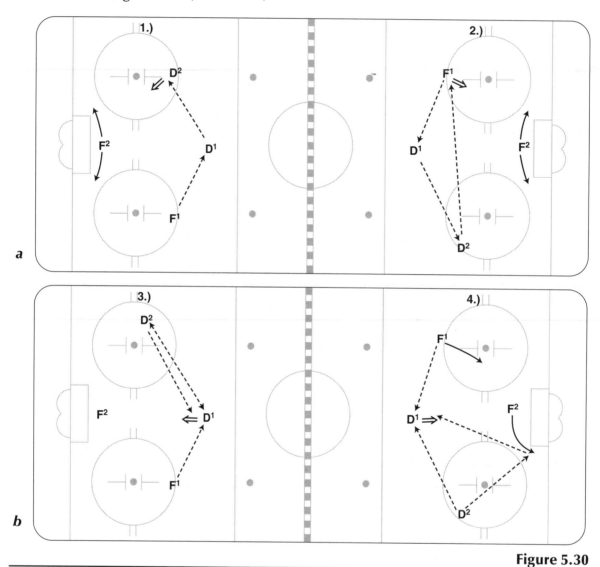

Figure 5.30

Part II

Defensive Play for Forwards and Defensemen

Chapter 6
Forechecking

There are basically three situations when a team would apply forechecking pressure. The most common is when a team dumps or chips the puck in from the neutral zone and then tries to retrieve it while the opponent tries to break out. The second is when the offensive team takes a shot that creates a rebound and then they forecheck to get the puck back. The final forechecking situation occurs off a turnover. When the offensive team turns the puck over they now need to apply forechecking pressure to get the puck back. Essentially, there are six keys to successful forechecking pressure:

1. F1 (the first forechecker in) must get in quickly and establish an angle when pursuing the puck carrier. This will limit the options for the breakout team. Taking away time and space from the breakout team forces hurried plays and mistakes. The quicker F1 responds to the puck the less time the offensive team will have to make a play.

2. Once the puck is moved, F1 must recover to a high position above the puck while F2 or F3 responds to pressure the pass. If F1 follows through on the hit he must get off the check right away and move above the circles while observing where the puck is and what is happening.

3. Continue to pressure and recover, pressure and recover until the puck is turned over. The response of the second and third player is key to keep heat on the opposition and force a turnover.

4. If the defensemen are going to pinch (pressure down the boards), they have to get to the puck before it is under control. Pinching defense must read the play and anticipate when the pass is being moved up to the wingers on the boards. One forward must always be in a position to back up the D. Having the high forward in a position to back up the pinching defense will prevent odd-man rushes the other way.

5. Good forecheckers use their sticks to take away passing lanes. Keep it on the ice and in the right lane. The "right lane" is the one that leads to the best breakout option for the other team. Take this option away, or make it difficult to make the pass by having an active stick.

6. Finish hits when appropriate. Physical play on the forecheck often forces the defense to move the puck quicker next time. There are times when a hit is not the best choice. When the forechecker is within striking distance of the pass then continue to pressure the puck instead of hitting the first opponent.

Forechecking Systems

This section describes five forechecking systems that a team can use to get the puck back. Which one you use may depend on the level you are coaching. For example, pressure forechecks work well against younger teams who have difficulty making quick decisions or sequential passes. It will also depend on the risk you want to take as a coach. More conservative coaches like to employ a system where one player is in on the forecheck but all other players are above the puck. More aggressive coaches will have their defense pinching on a regular basis. Once again, the key is proper execution. Therefore, any of the five systems could be used from novice to pro.

1-2-2 Forecheck

This forecheck involves hard pressure from the first forward (F1), and then as the puck is moved, quick pressure from F2 or F3 while F1 recovers. When F1 initiates pressure, he should angle the puck carrier in order to provide F2 and F3 a read on where the puck may go. Some coaches like F1 to stop the puck carrier from getting the back of the net and turn him up the boards, while other coaches encourage F1 to angle—steer and get a hit to separate the puck from the puck carrier. If F1 pressures the puck carrier and the puck is moved in the direction he is skating, then he should avoid finishing the hit and continue on to pressure the pass. Usually in a 1-2-2 system, the defensemen never pinch on direct passes to the opposing wingers but will come down on long wide-rim plays (where the breakout team rims the puck from one corner to the other half boards). F2 and F3 should be wide to initially take away passes to the boards and then react to mid-ice passes as they happen (figure 6.1).

The strength of this system is that the other team is enticed to bring the puck up the boards, and then the boards are taken away. Also if the opponent breaks out, usually only one forechecker is committed deep in the zone. The weakness in the 1-2-2 system is that the opponent has slightly more time to make plays on the breakout, and teams with good passing defensemen can hit the middle of the ice.

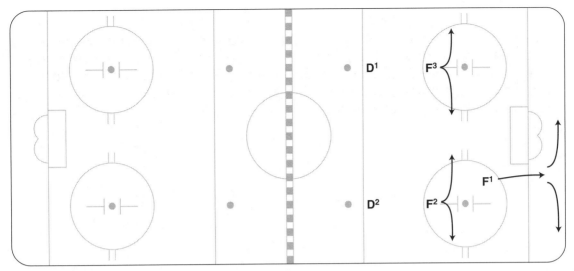

Figure 6.1 The basic 1-2-2 forecheck.

As mentioned in the breakout section, there are four ways the opponent can break out, so it is important when discussing forechecking systems to outline how to shut down each breakout. Listed here are the various breakout options and the specifics of how to react when forechecking in a 1-2-2 formation.

Up

F1 pressures O1. F2 and F3 position themselves in line with the dots, even with the opposing wingers and ready to take away passes up the boards. Initially, the wingers can also line up wider to prevent any quick rim plays, but we prefer that they stay inside to minimize mid-ice space and then move to an outside position. If O1 passes to O4, then F2 closes quickly and F3 moves across, locking the middle (preventing passes to the center) (figure 6.2).

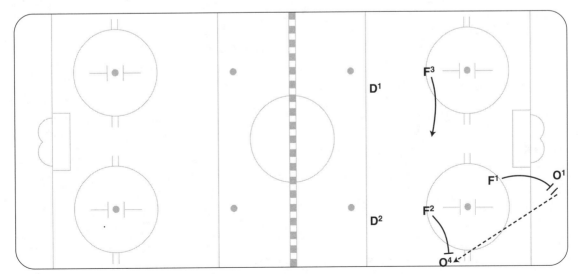

Figure 6.2 The 1-2-2 forecheck versus up.

Over

F1 pressures O1, and on the pass, F3 moves down to take away the pass to O2. F2 moves across to take away the pass up to O5. F1 recovers quickly and locks the middle (figure 6.3). If the puck is moved in the same direction while F1 is chasing O1, then F1 should continue to pressure 02 while F2 and F3 hold their positions.

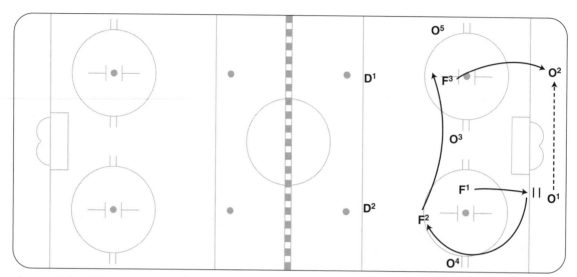

Figure 6.3   The 1-2-2 forecheck versus over.

Wheel

F1 forces O1 as he wheels the net while F2 locks across the middle. F3 backs up while staying inside the dots and is ready to take away the boards. F1 should force only if he is within one stick length of O1. If not, he should cut across the front of the net and pick up O1 on the other side (figure 6.4).

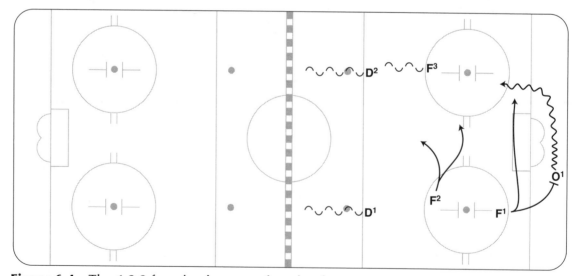

Figure 6.4   The 1-2-2 forecheck versus the wheel.

Reverse

F1 forces O1 as he wheels the net, and then as O1 reverses the puck, F2 closes on the pass. F3 moves across to lock the middle. It is important that F1 recover high on the back side (figure 6.5).

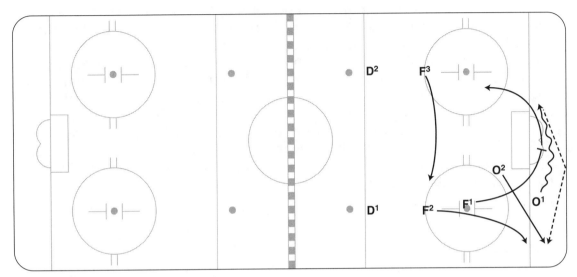

Figure 6.5 The 1-2-2 forecheck versus a reverse.

Rim

F1 pressures O1. If the puck is rimmed to the wide side, then D2 moves down to pinch on the winger. F3 covers up for D2 by moving up to the corner of the blue line. If the puck is rimmed up the strong side, then F2 closes down on the winger (figure 6.6).

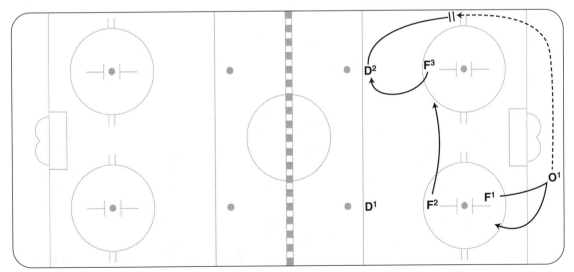

Figure 6.6 The 1-2-2 forecheck versus a rim.

2-1-2 Forecheck

This type of forechecking system was made famous by the Edmonton Oilers of the 1980s, who used their high-powered attack to pressure teams hard and recover the puck. This system forces the opponent's defense to handle pressure while also taking away all options up the boards. This is also a physical forecheck because F1 and F2 are in deep and looking to finish hits while the defense are set to come down the boards when the puck is moved to the opposition wingers. The 2-1-2 forecheck forces teams to use the middle of the ice to escape the zone. The strength of the system is in the pressure it applies while at the same time giving the opponent only certain areas to break out of the zone. The weakness of the 2-1-2 system is that at times you have a defenseman pinching and a forward back on defense accepting the rush when the opponent breaks out. Most forwards are weaker at defending the rush than any of the six defensemen. Figure 6.7 shows the details of the system.

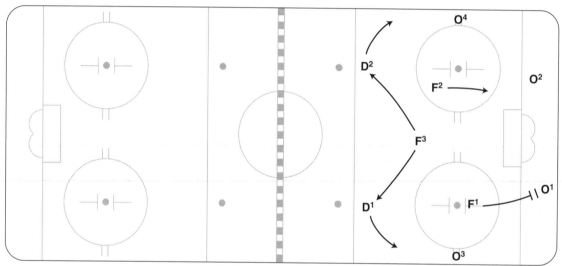

Figure 6.7   The basic 2-1-2 forecheck.

F1 pressures O1 to put the puck up the boards or across to his partner. F1 generally will have an opportunity to finish his hit on O1. Once the puck is moved and F1 has finished the hit, he recovers on the same side of the ice. F2 moves down on the weak side, anticipating a pass to O2. If the puck is moved up to O4, then F2 starts to recover on the same side.

F3 maintains a high position between the two defensemen. When D1 or D2 pinches down on a pass, then F3 moves out to the blue line on that side and backs up the D. If the opposition starts to break out, then F3 will have to back up like a defenseman. F3 is available in a solid defensive position, but once the puck is turned over, he is ready to receive a pass in the prime scoring area. At times F3 will move in offensively. As a result, when the puck is turned over, F2 or F1 may rotate into this position.

Both defensemen must read the play and anticipate when the puck may move up the boards. Once they see a pass is being made, they should pinch down (move toward the winger quickly, not letting him get by) on the winger. Finish hits on the winger but remain in control. When the puck moves away, get back to the blue line. Sometimes coaches talk about a pre-pinch position where the defensemen are one-third of the way down the boards when the puck is on that side. This makes the distance to pinch on the winger much shorter.

Listed below are the various breakout options and the specifics of how to react when forechecking in a 2-1-2 formation

Up

F1 pressures O1 to move the puck up the boards (figure 6.8). F2 moves down half way on the wide side ready to close on O2. F3 stays in the middle of the ice. D1 moves down quickly on the pass to 03. F3 fills in for D1.

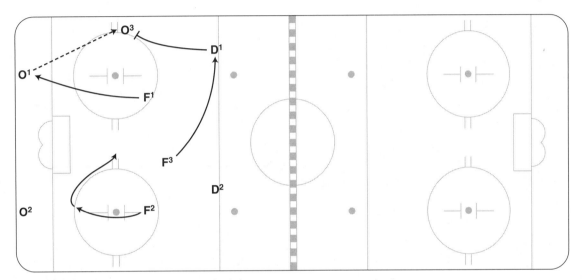

Figure 6.8 The 2-1-2 forecheck versus up.

Over

F1 pressures O1, and on the pass, F2 closes quickly on O2 (figure 6.9). If O2 passes the puck up the boards to the winger then D2 moves in and finishes the hit on 04 while F3 fills in on the blue line. If O2 tries to pass to the middle of the ice then F3 takes away O5.

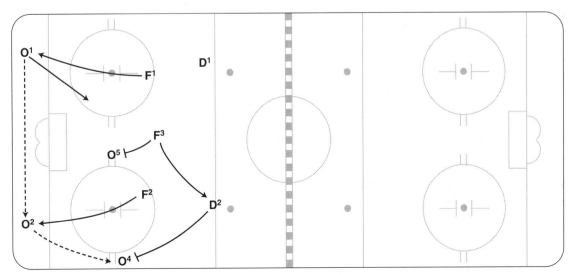

Figure 6.9 The 2-1-2 forecheck versus over.

Wheel

F1 forces O1 as he wheels the net while F2 moves down to prevent O1 from rounding the net and makes him pass to the boards (figure 6.10). D2 closes down on the board pass while F3 fills in on the blue line.

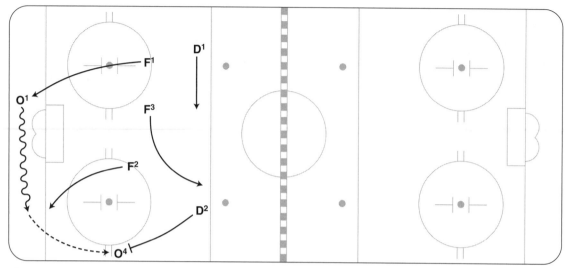

Figure 6.10   The 2-1-2 forecheck versus the wheel.

Reverse

F1 forces O1 as he wheels the net (figure 6.11). F2 is ready to stop O1 from wheeling and then once he sees the reverse to O2 moves in quickly to that side. F3 takes away the middle ice pass and is also ready to fill in for D1 if he pinches on a pass to the boards.

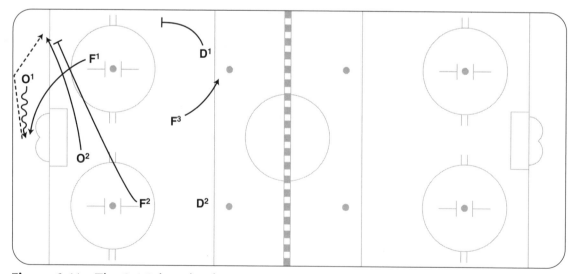

Figure 6.11   The 2-1-2 forecheck versus a reverse.

Rim

F1 pressures O1. If the puck is rimmed to the wide side, then D2 moves down to pinch on the winger (figure 6.12). F3 covers up for D2 by moving up to the corner of the blue line. If the puck is rimmed up the strong side, then D1 pinches with F3 once again filling in.

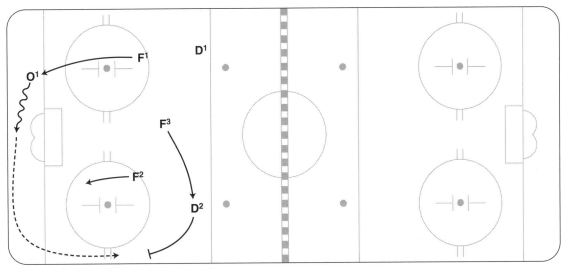

Figure 6.12   The 2-1-2 forecheck versus a rim.

2-3 System or Left-Lane Lock

In the 2-3 system, the key component is the pressure exerted by F1 and F2. They pressure the defensemen and each pass by skating constantly, finishing hits, and recovering quickly. The harder they work, the more hits they finish, and the quicker they recover, the more effective the system is. The 2-3 system is often referred to as the left-lane lock because one forward (F3) stays back on the left side of the ice—eliminating breakouts up those boards. The reason the left side was originally picked is because left wingers are traditionally better defensively than right wingers, while right wingers are traditionally the scorers. The defensemen shift to the right side, with the left D playing in mid-ice and the right D playing the right boards (figure 6.13).

Once the puck is turned over, the left winger can move in offensively, but then he has to move back when the puck is in doubt or turned over. The "lock" player doesn't always have to be the left winger; teams may decide to always use their top defensive player there or use a reading system where the left side is filled at any time by the closest player. Often it is better to designate one player to have this responsibility. If you don't designate exactly who should be in this position, most times you will have confusion with the read and end up with no one there, two players there, or players moving to the area late. Listed below are the various breakout options and the specifics of how to react when forechecking in a 2-3 or Left Lane Lock System.

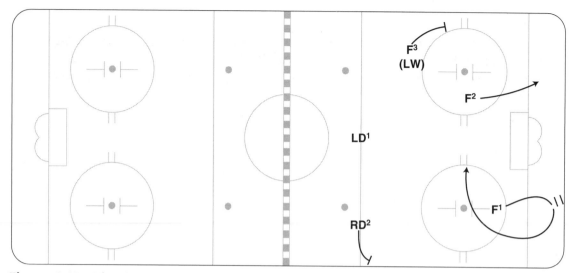

Figure 6.13   The 2-3 system or left-lane lock.

Up

F1 pressures O1 to move the puck up the boards (figure 6.14). F2 moves down ½ way on the wide side way ready to close on O2. F3 is on the far boards. D2 is in mid ice. D1 moves down quickly on the pass to O3. D2 covers up for D1 and F3 fills in wide on the blueline.

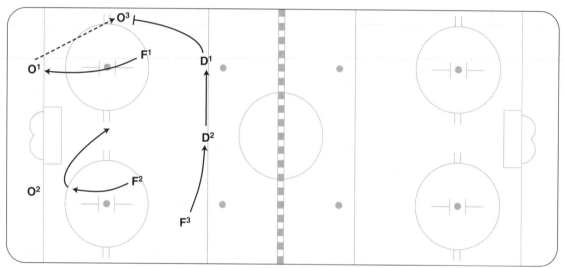

Figure 6.14   The 2-3 versus up.

Over

F1 pressures O1, and on the pass, F2 closes quickly on O2 (figure 6.15). If O2 passes the puck up the boards to the winger then F3 moves in and finishes the hit on O4 while D2 fills in on the blue line. D1 moves to mid ice.

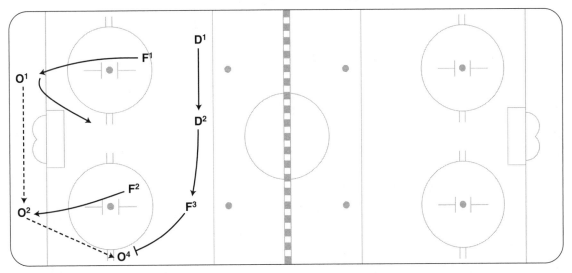

Figure 6.15   The 2-3 versus over.

Wheel

F1 forces O1 as he wheels the net while F2 moves down to prevent O1 from rounding the net and makes him pass to the boards (figure 6.16). F3 closes down on the board pass while D2 fills in on the blue line and D1 moves to mid ice.

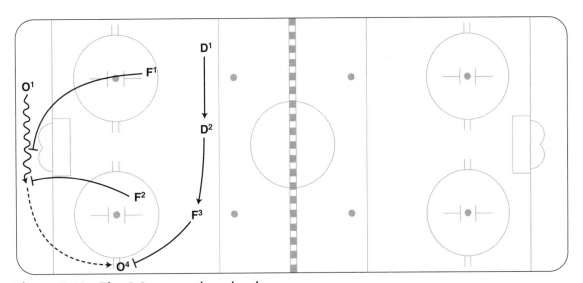

Figure 6.16   The 2-3 versus the wheel.

Reverse

F1 forces O1 as he wheels the net (figure 6.17). F2 is ready to stop O1 from wheeling and then once he sees the reverse to O2 moves in quickly to that side. D1 takes away any pass to the strong-side boards. D2 fills in if D1 pinches on a pass and F3 stays in mid ice on the blue line.

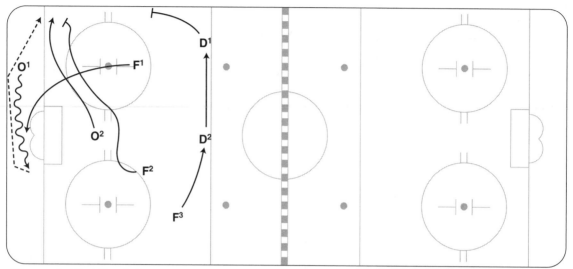

Figure 6.17   The 2-3 versus a reverse.

Rim

F1 pressures O1. If the puck is rimmed to the wide side, then F3 moves down to pinch on the winger (figure 6.18). D2 covers up for F3 by moving up to the corner of the blue line. If the puck is rimmed up the strong side, then D1 pinches with D2 once again filling in.

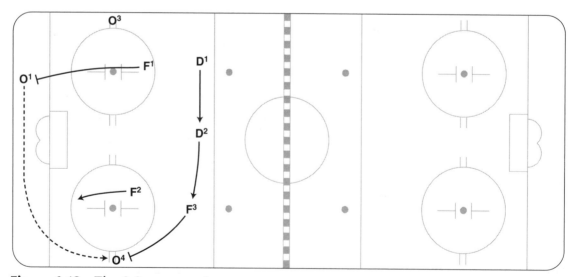

Figure 6.18   The 2-3 versus a rim.

Torpedo System

This interesting system was developed in Sweden and is not as commonly used in North America. It is very similar to the left-wing lock system but different in strategy.

The system is called *torpedo* because the first two forwards in on the forecheck buzz from corner to corner, pressuring the puck. The third forward (F3), who is usually the center, stays high on one side. The defensive defenseman stays in the center of the blue line and is more of a safety. On the opposite side of F3 is the offensive defenseman. The offensive defenseman and the center have the freedom to pinch down hard on all passes up their boards and also move in offensively when F1 and F2 have puck possession. Some coaches will allow F3 and D2 to pinch all the way down the boards to the goal line on that side (figure 6.19).

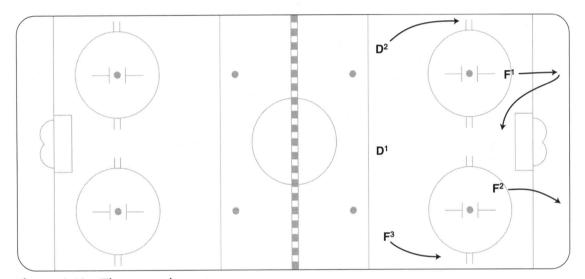

Figure 6.19   The torpedo system.

The advantage of this system is that F1 and F2 always provide pressure on the opposing defense, while passes up the boards are shut down by F3 and D2. Also when the puck is turned over, there are two potential passing options for F1 and F2. Offensively, F3 and D2 are always ready to jump in to receive a pass or take a shot. For this system to work effectively, the center (F3) must be good at playing back defensively because if D2 gets caught in the zone, F3 will have to play defense with D1. Few teams are as comfortable with their centers playing back as they are with their defense. Also the wingers who get in on the forecheck must be good, quick skaters who can "buzz" from side to side. As with other systems, the weakness in the torpedo system is that the middle of the ice is available for breakout plays. Although the torpedo is nontraditional and sometimes disregarded because of that, if you have the personnel to fit the descriptions of the positions, it is definitely worth trying.

Diagrams and descriptions for the breakout options have not been included here because the rotations are the same as 2-3 System. The one variation is that the center is back on the far side and the outside players F3 and D1 pinch very aggressively on any passes up the boards.

They even try to anticipate the pass being made and pinch early, not giving the wingers any opportunity to get the puck.

Control Forecheck

A control forecheck is used when the opposing players are set up behind their net with full control of the puck. This may happen off a line change or when the opponent gains the net and stops before you can apply pressure. Usually it doesn't make sense to force them out from behind the net because you will lose one forechecker and they will have an easy escape. The only exception to this would be if the first forchecker can get in to flush the defenseman quickly and surprise him before the other team has time to get organized. Once the opponent stops behind the net, there are a couple of ways to forecheck off the control setup.

Deep Trap

Much like the neutral zone forecheck, all five players back up and meet the attack at the blue line. F1 takes a shallow angle and steers the puck carrier to one side. The forward on that side (F2) stands up and denies the team from gaining the red line. F3 can lock across or stay wide. This is a more conservative strategy that forces opponents to move through the neutral zone against a lot of traffic with five defenders in this area. The opposition will have time and space to build up speed, but once they hit the blue line it will be taken away, and turnovers often result (figure 6.20).

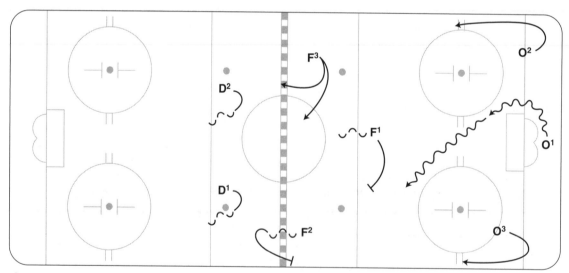

Figure 6.20   The deep trap.

Swing With Speed

Most offensive teams on a control breakout will swing one player behind the net with speed and stretch at least one other player. One way to neutralize this speed is to swing either the center or one of the wingers with their forward going behind the net. In this case, F1 backs out and lets F2 swing in with a good angle to take away the forward going behind the net.

If the player going behind the net is moving the other way, then F3 would move in. If the opposing D holds onto the puck and moves out from behind the net, now F3 would move in on an angle to force the puck carrier to one side. The defense must be aware of any stretch players because it is important to eliminate the threat of the long stretch pass. This control forecheck is effective in eliminating opposition speed but does open up some areas of the ice for them to make plays. The defenders are stretched out more than in the deep trap (figure 6.21).

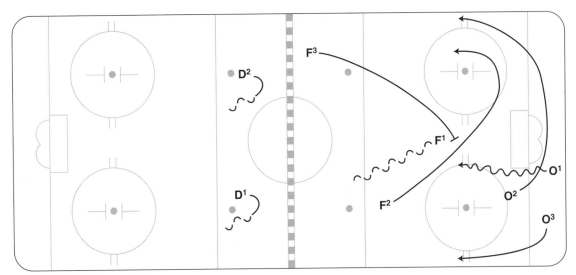

Figure 6.21   Swing with speed.

Chapter 7

Neutral Zone Forechecking and Backchecking

The neutral zone has changed dimensions over the last several years, which has dramatically altered the way teams defend this area. At almost all levels and in most leagues, the two-line pass is now allowed which opens up new options in this zone. Breakout teams are able to move the puck to the far blue line from behind their own net and while skating up ice can move the puck at any time to the far blue line (figure 7.1). Teams and coaching staffs are constantly talking about how much pressure they want to apply versus how passive they want to be. There is a lot of space to cover, so it is a double-edged sword. If you pressure, opponents have less time and may make mistakes, or they may take advantage of the extra space to work with. Conversely if you sit back, opponents have more time to read and make a play, but they have less space to work with. What do you do? Coaches have several options when designing the neutral zone forecheck.

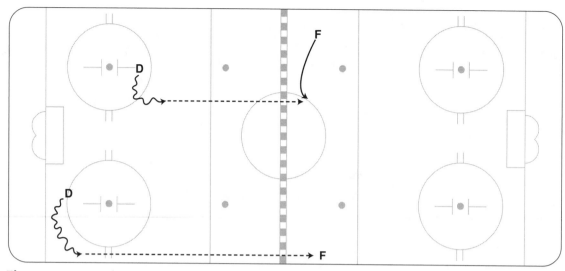

Figure 7.1   Breakout teams can now move the puck at any time to the far blue line.

Neutral Zone Forechecking

All neutral zone forechecking systems must have the ability to shift quickly as the puck moves from one side to the other. The key player is F1 with regard to his angle and stick placement. With his stick on the ice and proper skating angles, F1 can take away passing lanes from the opposition and steer them into a space where they don't want to go. F1 can also move the stick into different lanes to actively take away options. When the puck is moving up ice and then back or passed from side to side, both defensemen must be very good at regaining their gap. Teams that tighten their neutral zone gap (the distance between the defending defensemen and the attacking forwards) create havoc for attacking forwards trying to enter the offensive zone. Another key skill of strong neutral zone forechecking teams is that all three forwards are able to skate backward and face the play to make their reads easier. It is important to practice this with all five defensive players moving in unison.

Neutral Zone Forechecking Systems

There are five forechecking systems that teams may employ: 1-2-2 wide; 1-3-1; 2-1-2; 1-2-2 mid-ice lock; and retreating 1-2-2. Each system is described and discussed in this section.

1-2-2 Wide

This is the simplest system to teach a team and is very effective in clogging up the neutral zone. The most important factor in making it work effectively is the play of F1. He should never forecheck too deep or too wide and give up mid-ice space. F1 should take a shallow angle and steer the puck carrier to one side. If a D-to-D pass is made by the opposition, then F1 reattacks on a shallow angle once again. F1 must stay within 6 feet (1.8 m) of the blue line when initiating the push and take away the mid-ice pass with a well-placed stick. Let the opposition have the return D-to-D pass. Essentially F1 remains between the dots through this sequence to once again take away mid ice space (figure 7.2).

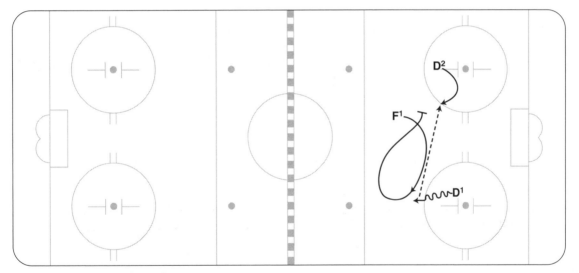

Figure 7.2   F1 angling the D-to-D pass.

F2 and F3 have simplified responsibilities. They stay on their side of the ice and lock the wide lanes (by staying in their specific lanes and skating backward to take away passing options). If the puck carrier comes up F2's side, then he stands up (doesn't back in) and keeps the opposition from gaining the red line (e.g., forces him to ice the puck). F3 takes the wide lane and makes sure no pass can get to a player in that lane. D1 and D2 keep a tight gap in the middle of the ice, ready to adjust to the puck (figure 7.3a). If the puck is moved to mid-ice or up the boards, then all five players react. D1 would overplay the boards when the puck comes up F2's side. D2 stays in mid ice and F3 takes the wide lane (figure 7.3b).

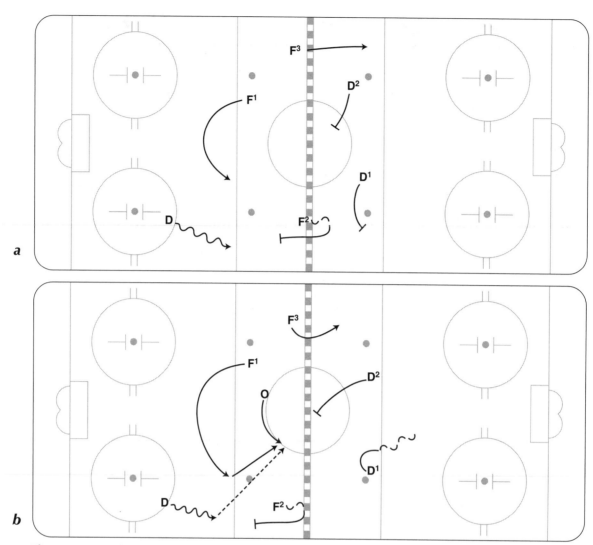

Figure 7.3 *(a)* D1 and D2 keep a tight gap in the middle of the ice ready to adjust to the puck. *(b)* If the puck is moved mid-ice or up the boards, all five players react.

1-3-1

European teams commonly used this system when they began playing without the red line, which was several years before it was removed in North America. Once the red line was removed there was now more space to cover and therefore this system was developed. When looking at the 1-3-1 the three 3 players across the middle of the ice definitely eliminate any room up the middle but gives up space behind on the far blue line. The theory is that it is more difficult to make the long pass especially through traffic. The 1-3-1 can be played in two ways, either by designating which defenseman is up in the middle of the ice or having the defensemen react depending on which side the puck is on. We believe it is easier if one D is designated as the up player and one D is designated as the back player (figure 7.4).

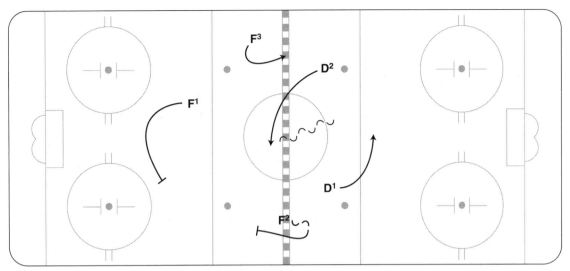

Figure 7.4   The 1-3-1 with one D as the up player and one D as the back player.

F1 has the freedom to go a little deeper (and press or angle the opponent with the puck) in this system because three lanes are covered in behind. F2 and F3 play their sides of the ice—if the puck carrier comes up F2's side, then he stands up and prevents him from gaining the red line. F3 makes sure the wide lane is locked up and also prevents any passes from going to players in behind D2.

D2 tightens up in the middle of the ice, playing as far up as the top of the circle. D2 may skate forward or accept the rush skating backward. Regardless, D2 must keep a tight gap in the middle. D1 sits back and plays like a rover in football—stays in the middle initially and then reacts to wherever the puck goes (figure 7.5).

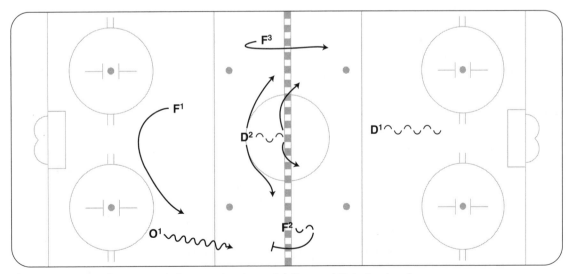

Figure 7.5   D2 keeps a tight gap in the middle and D1 sits back.

2-1-2

This is a common neutral zone forecheck off a lost draw, but it is also used effectively by many teams who want to apply more pressure in this area (when trailing in the game or in need of a more offensive approach). The 2-1-2 system is one of the more aggressive neutral zone forechecks. It is basically a man-on-man system in the neutral zone. F2 and F3 attack the opponent's defense in a staggered fashion. Therefore if O1 has the puck, F2 will force and F3 will be halfway to O2. If a pass is made to O2, then F3 will jump immediately. F1 locks onto the other team's center, making sure no passes can be made to the middle of the ice, because both defensemen have outside responsibility. D1 moves up on any passes to O4, and D2 does the same for passes to O5. It is important that one D remain in the middle of the ice at all times when the other D is forcing the outside. (figure 7.6).

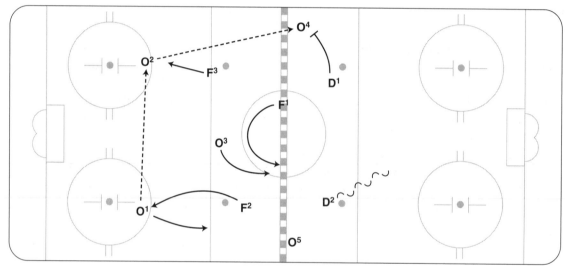

Figure 7.6   The 2-1-2 forecheck.

1-2-2 Mid-Ice Lock

This system is common at many levels because it denies teams the ability to bring the puck up the middle and forces teams to move the puck wide and try to enter up the boards. F1 starts by steering the puck to one side, and unlike other systems mentioned, he may take away either the D-to-D return pass or the wide-lane pass, depending on which is a priority (figure 7.7). This will influence the angle F1 takes and also the position of his stick. F2 challenges O1 before the red line, forcing him to ice the puck or chip in behind. F3 locks across hard on the opposing player in mid-ice. F3 does not allow passes to any player in mid-ice and forces the opposition to make the long, wide pass to gain entry to the offensive zone.

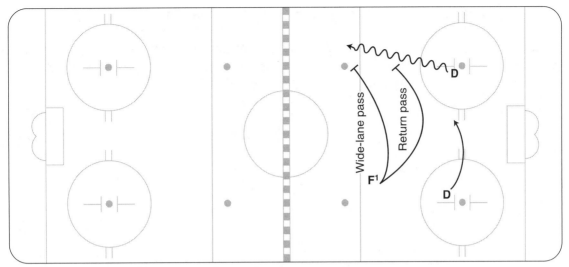

Figure 7.7   The F1 taking away the wide or return pass.

D1 is ready to recover any chips in behind F2 and ready to challenge any bank passes to O3. D2 is responsible for any wide passes to O4. D2 must be alert because this is the one way teams try to break the 1-2-2 mid-ice lock—they will pass wide to O4 and try to have him pick up speed before the pass is made (figure 7.8).

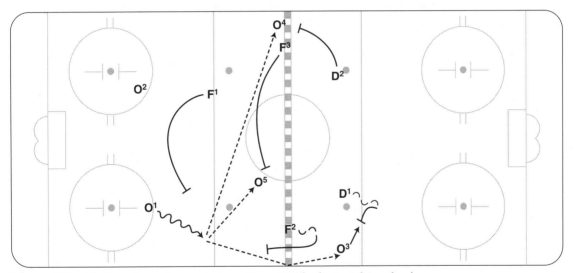

Figure 7.8   Defending all passing options with the mid-ice lock.

Retreating 1-2-2

This is a very defensive setup and is similar to the 1-2-2 mid-ice lock. The primary difference is that all five players tighten up, with F1 moving down to the top of the offensive zone circles and the two defensemen back no farther than the center red line. As the offensive team advances up ice, all five players skate backward and retreat in a tight pack (figure 7.9*a*).

This creates the visual of limited space for the offensive team. F2 and F3 initially remain wide but align themselves with the dots giving up space along the boards and taking away space inside. D1 and D2 must be aware of the long stretch pass. A pass to the outside is not dangerous, but they have to protect against being too wide and allowing the long mid-ice pass.

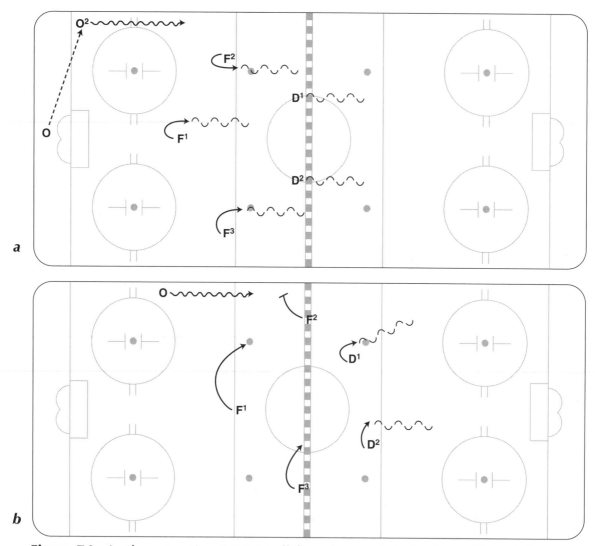

Figure 7.9   In the retreating 1-2-2 *(a)* all five players skate backward in a tight group. *(b)* F1 angles the puck carrier as soon as the puck advances above the offensive circles.

F1 starts to angle the puck carrier as soon as the puck advances above the offensive circles (figure 7.9*b*). Once again F1 takes a shallow angle at the puck carrier and tries to steer the puck up one side of the ice. F1 stays between the dots, allowing the puck carrier to move into the trap. F2 will now stand up from the inside out, taking away the red line so the puck carrier cannot dump the puck in. F3 starts to lock across the middle and is ready to take away any passes to that area. D1 stays in behind F2 in case the puck gets chipped to the far blue line. D2 stays back in mid-ice but is ready to confront any wide-lane passes. All five players should move like there is a rope tying them together.

Neutral Zone Backchecking

Every team wants to be known as a hardworking team. Well, there is nothing more reflective of a team's work ethic than the players' willingness and commitment to backcheck. The backcheck starts once the puck is turned over in the offensive zone and doesn't end until either puck possession has been regained or you shift into defensive zone coverage. All three forwards need to be involved in the backcheck. Some teams rely mainly on one backchecker, with the other two forwards coasting back and watching that the other team's Ds don't jump by them. This strategy allows for quick counterattacks using long stretch passes once the puck is turned over, but it does not result in as many turnovers as when all three forwards come back hard. Also it provides the offensive team with more space to work with as they advance up the ice.

The backcheck is set up in the offensive zone off the forecheck when players away from the puck recover above the puck to reattack (figure 7.10a),

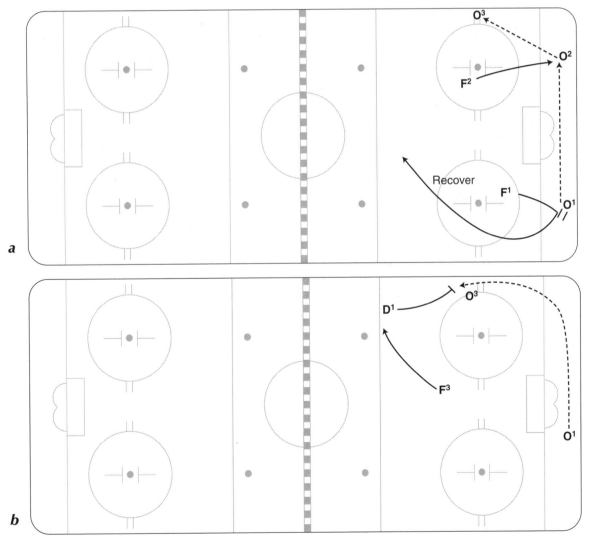

Figure 7.10   The back check set up by (a) recovering or (b) backing up a pinching defense (continued on next page).

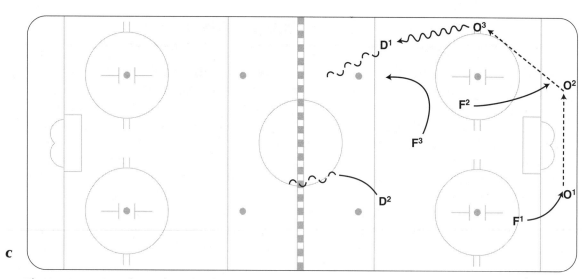

Figure 7.10 (continued)   The back check set up by *(c)* being in a high offensive position.

back up a pinching defenseman (figure 7.10*b*), or initiate the backcheck by being in a high offensive position (figure 7.10*c*, above). It is important that players in the offensive zone recognize the potential for loss of possession and quickly get themselves into an appropriate backchecking position.

Late in games, a strong F3 (high forward) position in the offensive zone is key to eliminating odd-man rushes against. This should be a strategy throughout the game. When in a high position F3 has two choices on how to force the breakout. The first is to immediately pressure the pass if he has support from a team mate who is recovering to the high slot. If he doesn't have support the second option is to "soft lock". This refers to F3 not going for a hit but angling the offensive player up ice (toward his own net) and running him out of room or making him hurry his pass (figure 7.11). In this way, he keeps in the rush and not behind it. If the offensive player makes a good pass up ice F3 is still in a great position to apply backchecking pressure and chase down the rush.

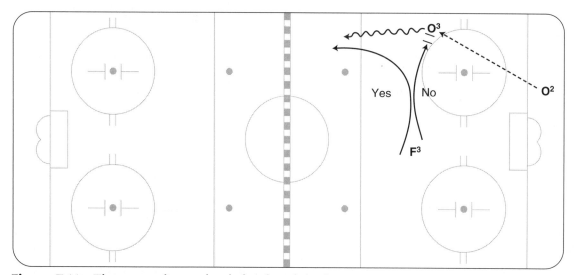

Figure 7.11   The neutral zone backcheck soft lock.

Let's discuss the keys to an effective backcheck.

○ Move into a high recovery position. First and probably most important is that all forwards on the forecheck move immediately into a high recovery position when the puck is moved away from them in the offensive zone or after they make a hit (figure 7.12). The high recovery area is the top of the circles in the offensive zone; that is where coaches always want the forwards to move to. By always having one forward in this area teams rarely give up odd man rushes. This now sets the stage for an effective backcheck. If the forwards don't get in the habit of recovering, then it won't matter what your backchecking strategy is because they will not be in a position to help out.

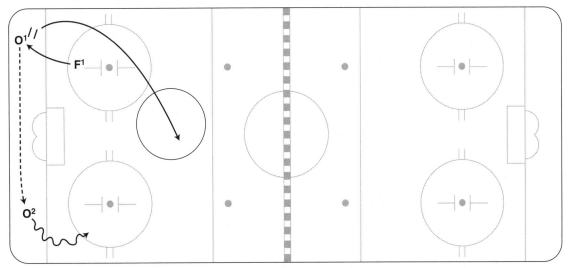

Figure 7.12   The high recovery area off a forecheck.

○ Pressure the attack from behind. All forwards come back hard through mid-ice. Backcheck hard, and prepare to move in transition with speed once the puck is turned over. Coaches must reinforce with their players that it is important for all three forwards to come back hard; not just the responsibility of the high forward or the closest forward (figure 7.13a).

○ Outnumber them at the line. Keep pressuring the attack from behind, and at the defensive blue line, you should outnumber the attacking team. Squeeze the attack from both sides, with the forwards pressing from behind and the Ds keeping a tight gap on the other side (figure 7.13b). If you were to look at an overhead picture of the opposition attack at your blue line, you should see more of the defending team than the offensive team. Show the team a freeze frame at the defensive blue line and if you have 5 players in the picture and the opponent has, three, then the players are doing a great job of squeezing the attack. Often the puck will be turned over in this area or the opposition will be forced to dump the puck in.

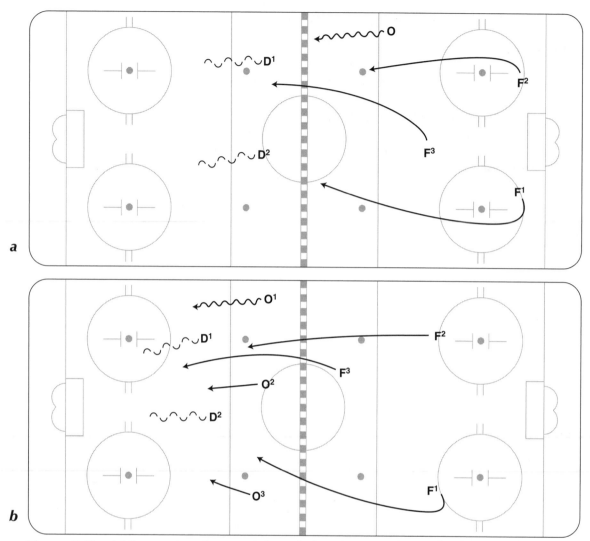

Figure 7.13   *(a)* Pressuring the attack from behind or *(b)* outnumbering them at the line.

○ Have set rules for F1 and D1. Make sure you have rules for which player plays the puck carrier once the play advances to your blue line and which player holds inside position. There are two ways to do this.

1. F1 pressures the puck carrier hard and if he can catch him before center does so and tries to turn the puck over. But after the center line he releases the puck carrier to the defense (D1), and now F1 holds inside position and supports the defense while looking for late players. D1 calls that he has the puck carrier and stands him up at the line, knowing he has inside protection form F1 (figure 7.14).

2. F1 pressures the puck carrier hard from behind and continues to try to steal the puck and keep the puck carrier wide all the way into the zone. D1 recognizes that this is the strategy and now holds inside position and supports F1 while looking for late players (figure 7.15).

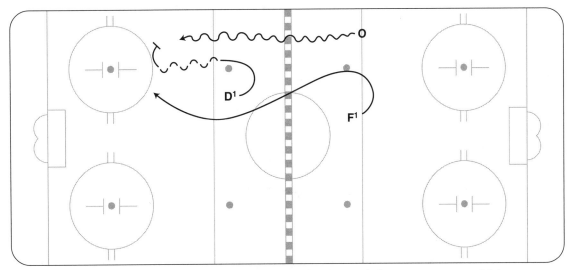

Figure 7.14   D1 stands the puck carrier up at the line while F1 protects mid-ice.

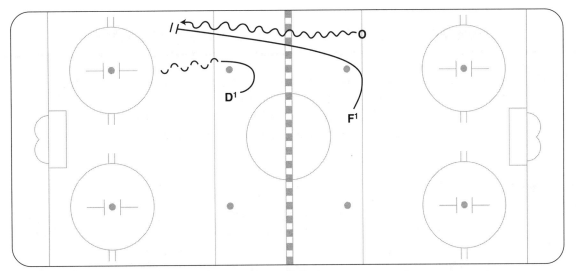

Figure 7.15   D1 holds the inside position while F1 pressures the puck carrier.

O Watch for stretch players. With no red line, the defense must be aware of the stretch player. Generally this is the responsibility of the defense, but at times and in certain systems such as the 1-3-1 or 1-2-2 wide neutral zone forecheck, it will be the responsibility of the wide forward. When forechecking or in possession of the puck in the offensive zone and the other team sends a player out early into the neutral zone, it is important that the closest D drop back in coverage and hold mid-ice. When covering a stretch player, you do not have to skate close to the player—just maintain mid-ice position and equal depth. If a quick pass is made up, make sure you have support before going out to play the stretch player. Do not allow the stretch player to bump the puck into mid-ice to create an odd-man rush (figure 7.16).

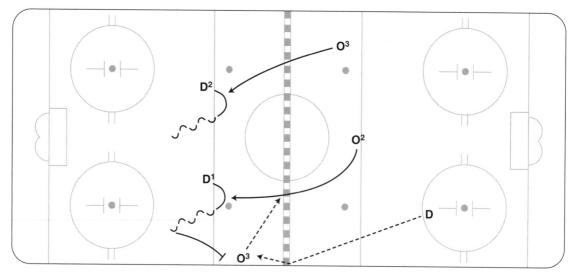

Figure 7.16   The stretch player bumping the puck into mid-ice as D1 overplays.

Neutral Zone Backchecking Systems

There are three backchecking systems that teams may employ: wide-lane lock, midlane backcheck, and hound the puck. Each system is described and discussed in this section, and each has a different emphasis on where the offensive players are confronted and how they are confronted.

Wide-Lane Lock

In this system, the first forward on the backcheck immediately moves to an outside lane. Once the forward gets into the wide lane, he may skate backward or forward but must always be able to see the puck and any opposing skater in that lane. This forward is responsible for any opposition player skating between the dots and the boards on that side. D1 now moves to mid-ice, assuming responsibility for this lane, and D2 takes the strong side where the puck carrier is. Essentially the ice is divided into three parts, with each of these players protecting a zone (figure 7.17). The offensive team will have a difficult time getting across the blue line in possession of the puck with three players protecting the line. All three defensive players (D1, D2, F1) attempt to stand the attack up at the blue line while F2 and F3 continue to pressure from behind the attacking players.

The responsibility of F1 is to prevent any passes to that side and to stay close to his check. It is always best to be deeper than the opponent, which is usually called good defensive side position.

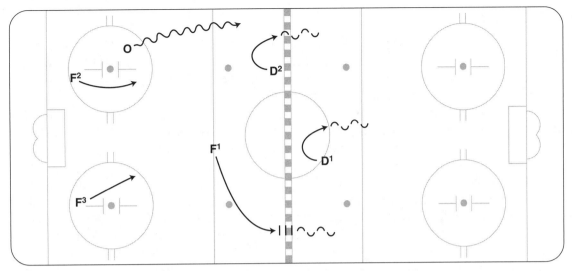

Figure 7.17   Neutral zone backchecking wide-lane lock.

Midlane Backcheck

Once the puck is turned over in this system, the first instinct of the high forward should be to get to mid-ice and come back hard through the center seam. All forwards come back through the middle, allowing the defensemen to play the outside areas. The first forward back protects the defensemen from being beaten inside by always staying between the puck and the net (figure 7.18). Therefore, if a defenseman makes a mistake, the forward is always in a position to cover up. Plus, having the forward in the middle intimidates the puck carrier and forces him to stay wide because of the lack of space inside.

When the first forward comes back through the middle, he should come all the way back to the low slot area and then move out to support the defense. The second and third backchecking forwards should once again come back hard—look around for any late players entering the zone, and stop at the top of the circles in good defensive position.

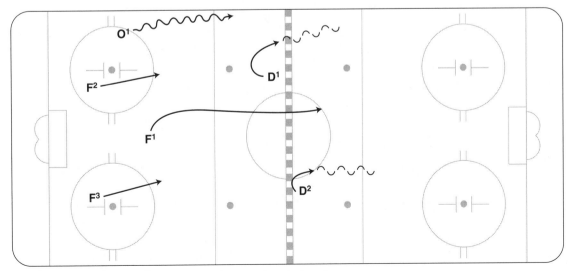

Figure 7.18   The midlane neutral zone backcheck.

Hound the Puck

This system is the opposite of the midlane backcheck. The first forward "hounds" the puck (backchecks toward the player with the puck) as hard as he can, and if a pass is made, then the forward continues to pressure the puck (figure 7.19). The forwards limit the time and space for the opposing players as they move through the neutral zone and the defense hold inside position—protecting the space between the dots. Coaches who like this system are generally ones who want to have a pressure philosophy and in all areas of the ice want to deny time and space.

The advantage of this system is that the opponent has little time with the puck through the neutral zone if the backchecking forwards are quick and work hard, plus the positioning of the defense is always inside. The disadvantage is that at times there is confusion between the backchecking forwards and the defense as to what to do if the forwards cannot catch the opposition by the blue line or confront the pass quickly enough. A team must develop rules for these two scenarios so there is no confusion when they occur. One rule involves hounding the puck until the red line, where the backchecking forward must then pick a lane to skate into or pick up a man to cover.

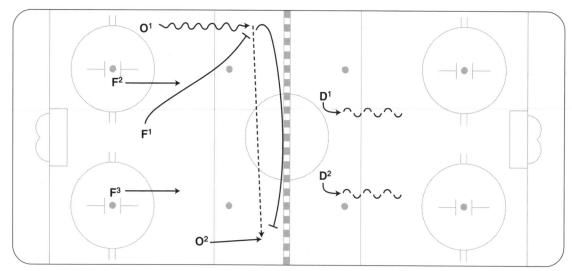

Figure 7.19   "Hounding" the puck in the neutral zone backcheck.

Chapter 8

Defensive Zone Entries

The most critical aspect of defensive zone entries is that the defensive players accepting the attack must correctly read the play. For the purposes of this book, defensive zone entries are defined as the moment the attacking team hits the offensive blue line with the puck. Once this happens, the defensive players, which are usually the defensemen and possibly one forward, must scan the rush quickly and identify how many attackers and how many defenders. Because of the dynamic nature of hockey, this read must be done in seconds, and rarely is any situation exactly like another. Once the defenders see the rush clearly, they should call out whether it is a two on one, two on two, or three on two and also communicate to any forwards coming back which player to pick up. The forwards coming back must read the rush quickly from the back side and pick up the right players.

If reads are so important, how do coaches improve the players' ability to identify the rush? Well, there are a couple of ways. First, do read-the-rush drills in practice, where players are faced with different situations; once they play it out, they get feedback from a coach who is off to the side. A simple read-the-rush drill may include a neutral zone regroup where the defenseman must step up, read the rush, close the gap, and make it difficult for the offensive team to gain entry with possession. Another drill starts as a two on two with a backchecker and turns into a three on three, with the coach sending the backchecking and offensive forwards at different intervals.

The second way to help players identify the rush is to review the video and ask what they see and how they would play each situation. Many times while watching video, players will comment that during the game they read that they have less time and space when in fact on the video they see it differently. It is helpful to hear their perspective. Also, during games have one coach on the bench who provides feedback and discusses reads with the players while the game is going on. The best approach is to ask the players, "What did you see on that rush?" and then tell them what you saw. Finally, to clear up any confusion about reads, set a rule for what players should do if they are unsure. The rule should be: hold mid-ice position, take a few more seconds to sort it out, and then when you are sure, move to outside areas to challenge the puck carrier.

Handling Defensive Zone Entries

Once the puck carrier crosses the line there are a number of options available to the offensive team as outlined in Chapter 3. To develop your team in the area of handling defensive zone entries you need to review each of these with them and how they are to execute, if facing that situation. Whether your team is faced with an attacker who delays, a two on one, two on two, or any variation of a three on two, three on three . . . they will know how to play it.

It is important to note here that for all entries described we focus primarily on the two defense and the first backchecking forward (figure 8.1). As mentioned in the backchecking chapter, the last two forwards coming back in the zone come back hard through mid-ice (inside the dots) and stop at the top of the circles in the defensive zone. Keep sticks on the ice to discourage passing options.

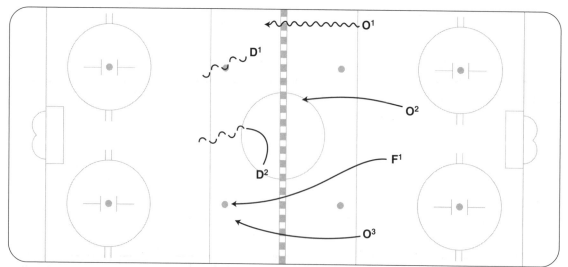

Figure 8.1 Handling the rush with two defense and a backchecking forward.

Delays

If the opposing forward delays when entering the offensive zone, first read whether the rush is even. If the offensive team outnumbers the defensive team, then the defense should hold inside position and wait for help. There are two ways to play an even rush where the puck carrier delays. D1 steps up and plays the puck carrier while F1 locks mid-ice and protects the space behind D1 (figure 8.2a). F1 looks for late players coming into the zone and D2 plays the middle to wide side area. D2 will automatically take any mid lane net drives. The second way to play an even-rush delay is to have the backchecking forward go after the puck carrier while both defenseman drop back inside with their sticks on the ice, ready to take away any plays inside and cover players going to the net (figure 8.2b). Either way is effective, but teams should pick one of these strategies and stick to it so that both the defense and forwards always know who is going to take the delay player and who is going to stay inside.

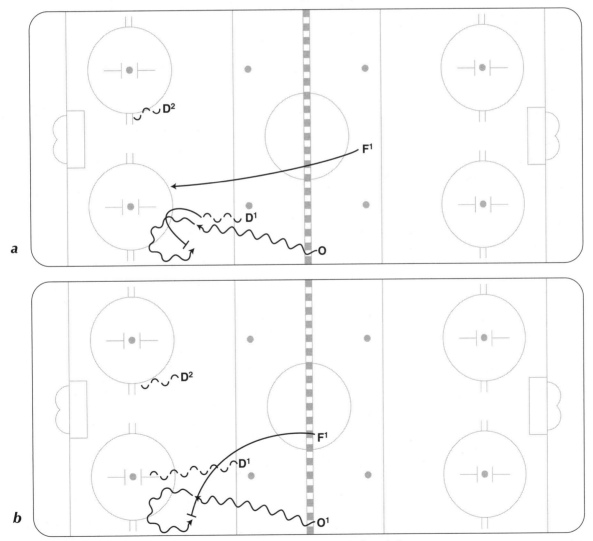

Figure 8.2   *(a)* D1 playing the delay. *(b)* F1 playing the delay.

Two on One

Coaches have several different theories about how to play a two on one, but there is no factual evidence to say which is better. First, the defenseman should stay in mid-ice regardless of whether the two on one is down the middle or wide. Early, try to push the puck carrier wide. Once the attack moves into the circles, the defenseman has two options:

1. Be responsible for the player without the puck, and leave the player with the puck to the goaltender. To execute this tactic the defense must turn to take the wide player at the last moment in order to minimize the risk of the opposition puck carrier cutting to a better shooting position. When the defense turns to take his check, he should still keep an eye on the puck carrier so he knows what is happening. The primary responsibility of the defenseman in this tactic is to make sure no pass can be made to the back door for an empty-net tap-in (figure 8.3a).

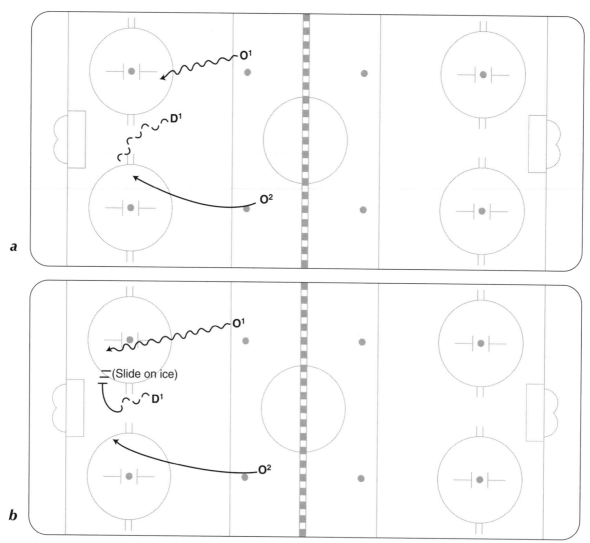

Figure 8.3 During the two on one the defenseman either *(a)* makes sure no pass can be made back door or *(b)* slides flat on the ice with feet facing the net to take away the passing option.

2. The second way to play a two on one is for the defense, to slide flat on the ice with feet facing the net to take away the passing option and force the puck carrier to shoot (figure 8.3b). This slide must be executed with proper timing. The problem with the slide is that until they perfect it many defensemen slide too far or leave their feet to early—allowing the puck carrier to cut in. Also once the defenseman sides he is in no position to defend a rebound.

Two on Two

In all two-on-two situations, the defensemen should make sure they have a tight gap. Without a tight gap, it is difficult to play the two on two properly. In order to maintain a tight gap defense should be constantly be reminded to "gap up" which means to move up with the play and tighten up on the rush. Keep two stick lengths as a reference point – any further back and the defense will lose the ability to move back at the same speed as the rush. There are two ways to play a two on two, and both have their strengths and weaknesses.

The first is for D1 to stay with the puck carrier regardless of what he does. If the puck carrier drives, delays, or cuts to the middle, then D1 stays with him and D2 keeps position on the other player. The strength in playing it this way is that there is no confusion as to who has whom, while the weakness is that sometimes the offensive team can lose coverage, especially when the puck carrier crosses with the second offensive player (figure 8.4a).

The other way to play a two on two is for D1 to take the puck carrier on the drive or delay but when the puck carrier crosses the ice, D1 leaves him for D2 to play. Now D1 picks up the other player (figure 8.4b). The disadvantage here is that D2 might not be in a strong position to pick up F1, and D2 might miss coverage on F2 in the exchange. The advantage is that both Ds always stay in good mid-ice position and know that they have their own side of the ice to cover.

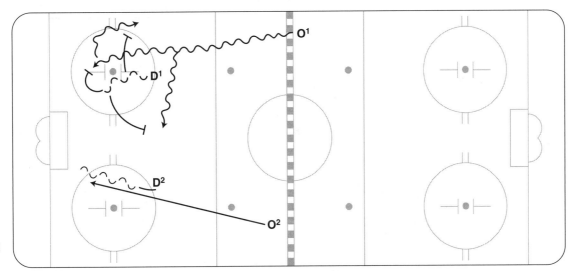

Figure 8.4 (a) In a two on two, one option is for D1 to stay with the puck carrier no matter what *(continued on next page)*.

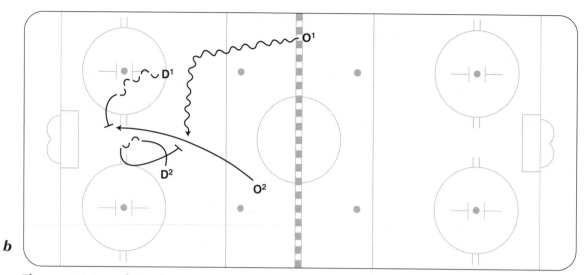

Figure 8.4 *(continued)*   In a two on two, a second option is for D1 to leave the puck carrier for O2.

Three on Two

When reading a three on two, both defensemen stay in mid-ice and try to delay the attack. Don't confuse what looks like a three on three for what really is a three on two. What I mean here is that at times the defense will say that "I thought the backchecker had the third player" but in reality the backchecker is a step away and couldn't catch the player. If the offensive team sends a back-side drive, the strong-side D1 now plays the two on one, and the back-side D2 goes with the drive (figure 8.5). If it is a midlane drive, the back-side D2 plays the two on one, trying to shade (commit to one player while ready to take the other player) the drive player but ready to come out on the wide pass. D1 plays the puck carrier.

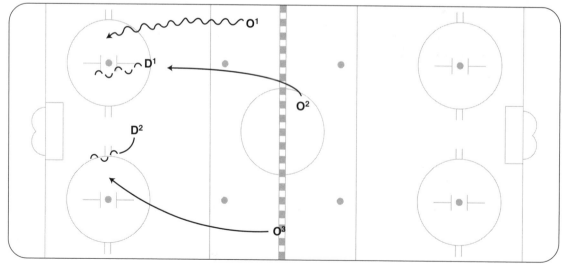

Figure 8.5   Defending a three on two back-side drive.

Three on Two With a Close Backchecker

In this situation the backchecker is close to catching the rush but doesn't have position on any of the offensive players (figure 8.6). D1 and D2 should play it as a three on two until the backchecker has caught the opposition's highest player. With the new obstruction rules not allowing the backchecker to hook the offensive player, do not play it like a three on three until the offensive player is clearly caught by the backchecker. Make sure the backchecker has body position on his player before the Ds adjust and play it as a three on three. It is better to play it safe until you are sure because as soon as one of the defense overplay the outside it could open up a two on one inside if the backchecker is not in position.

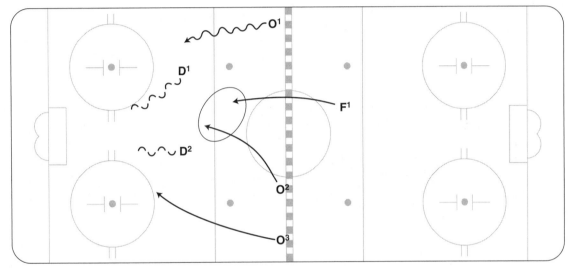

Figure 8.6   A three on two with a close backchecker.

Three on Three

The backchecker must identify the player he is covering. As outlined in the backchecking chapter (pages 118-120), some teams like their backchecker in the wide lane and some like him in the mid-ice lane, so the defensemen adjust according to the team's system. Usually the backchecker will take the highest player unless he is already in position to take the wide player. Keep your stick off the body of the free player so you don't take a penalty and get good body position. Good body position is where you are close enough to the player to take his stick and at the same time keep an eye on where the puck is (figure 8.7).

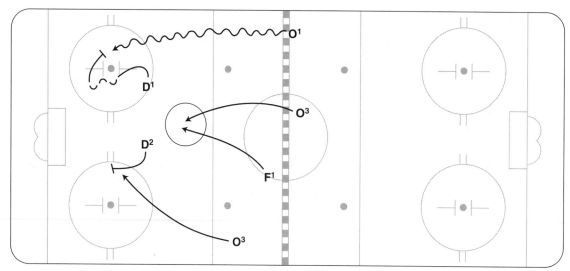

Figure 8.7 The backchecker taking the highest player.

If the backchecker is coming back through mid-ice, he should leave any drive players to the defense and pick up the higher areas. Therefore if the middle offensive player drives the net looking for a pass or deflection then this player would be covered by D2. F1 must look around for the third forward and move to check him. Sometimes F1 will have to overplay the outside area if this forward is wider. As the play gets below the circles, he should lock onto his check (figure 8.8).

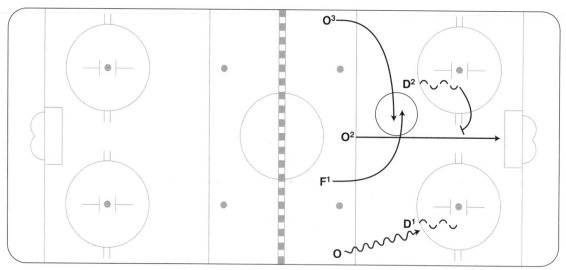

Figure 8.8 The backchecker leaving the drive and taking the highest player.

If the team's neutral zone system has the first forward back locking the wide lane (figure 8.9), then on three-on-three rushes the forward should stay with the player in this lane, and the defensemen will adjust to cover the middle and strong side. This becomes more of a man on man coverage when the play enters the defensive zone.

Finally, if the backcheckers are instructed to hound the puck, then with all three-on-three rushes the backchecking forward will usually have the strong side while D1 will shift to the middle and D2 will take the wide or backside lane.

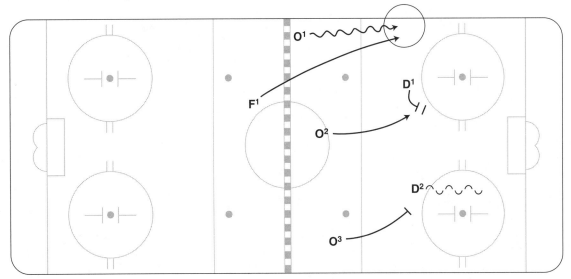

Figure 8.9   The three on three if the team's neutral zone has the first forward back locking the wide lane.

Chapter 9
Defensive Zone Coverage

Defensive zone coverage refers to coverage once the offensive team has set up in the zone and all five defensive players are also in the zone . . . this may happen off a face-off in the defensive zone, after the opposition enters the zone and takes a shot on net, or when the opposition enters the zone and maintains puck possession for several seconds. Following are some key principles to remember in defensive zone coverage:

○ **Maintain mid-ice positioning.** Players are often in such a hurry to get to the outside to apply pressure to the puck carrier that they over commit and leave space in the most dangerous scoring area—the low slot. Few goals are scored from this outside area but in a lot of teams defensive play they will be caught with too many players covering the outside space. At younger levels often two players will go at the puck carrier not seeing that the other has already committed. Once players understand the value of mid ice positioning they will be less anxious to jump. It is important to pressure the puck carrier to deny time and space but only one person at a time.

○ **Stay between the puck and the net.** When checking players, make sure you always have great defensive side positioning by staying in a direct line between the puck and the net (figure 9.1). Support players defensively down low below the dots should always be on this line from the puck to the net.

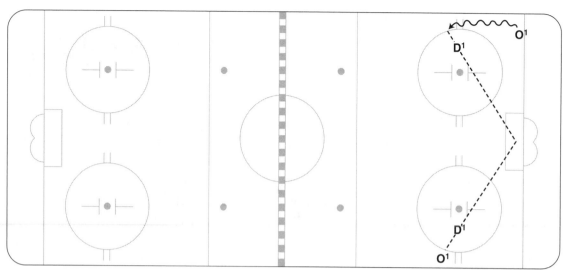

Figure 9.1   Great defensive side positioning requires staying in a direct line between the puck and the net.

○   **Be ready to block shots.** In today's game, it is much more common for defenders to get into shooting lanes and block shots (primarily with the legs) or discourage opposing players from taking a shot. Although blocking a shot hurts, it takes away good scoring chances. Players who sacrifice their body to block a shot are respected by teammates and coaches. There are times when a player sprawls to block a shot which requires timing but most of the shots that are blocked are by players who make themselves big in shooting lanes. Many teams include blocking shots as part of regular practice routines.

○   **Keep your stick on the ice.** In offensive situations, coaches often remind players, "Keep your stick on the ice, and be ready for the pass." We believe this is even more important in the defensive zone. By having your stick on the ice, you take away passing lanes and often intercept pucks. When you look at a video clip of all five defensive players with their sticks on the ice, it is amazing how much more space is covered. Although you often see players holding their sticks up in a comfortable position, their hands at their hips, this is a bad habit.

○   **See the puck, see your man.** It is important in all sports for defenders to be able to see where the offensive player is and where their coverage responsibility is. Keep your head on a swivel and look back and forth between the two, because the position of the puck is changing while at the same time your check is moving.

○   **Find the stick on rebounds.** When the puck is shot on goal and there is a rebound, defensive players often try to find the puck, and the free offensive player finds it first and scores. First cover the opponent's stick, and then look to respond to the loose puck. The goaltender should tell the defensive players where the puck is (in the corner... in your feet). This will help defenders respond once they have covered the stick and taken away any immediate rebound chances. Some defense also make the mistake of trying to knock the player down in front. When the puck is in the net area the first rule is to take a stick. Next it is important to get body position on the player and finally you may attempt to move the player or knock him down. These principles will all be reviewed in the following systems.

Defensive Zone Systems

There are several systems a team could use in their defensive zone. Teams may choose between the 2-3 system, low zone collapse, half ice overload, or man on man coverage. The 2-3 system should be used against teams that have a balanced attack in the offensive zone while the low zone collapse works well against teams who have trouble generating chances from their defense but generate a lot of chances from below the circles. The half ice overload smothers the offensive team on one side of the ice but with teams who are good at changing the point of attack it is not as effective. The man-on-man system is based on pressure and sticking to your check. If one player loses their check then excellent scoring opportunities result. It is not our recommendation that coaches should change from system to system depending on the opponent. We believe it is important to pick one that is suitable for your level of play and teach it well.

2-3 System

In this system, the two defensemen work with one forward (usually the center) to cover down low, while the wingers cover the slot and higher areas (figure 9.2). Listed here are the key areas of defensive zone coverage, including teaching points for coaches. This should form a basis for teaching your players how to play in your own zone without the puck. It can also be used as a framework for developing your defensive zone drills. While in the defensive zone, all players should have an "active stick," meaning the stick is on the ice and it is moving. This takes away shooting lanes and leads to turnovers and transition opportunities.

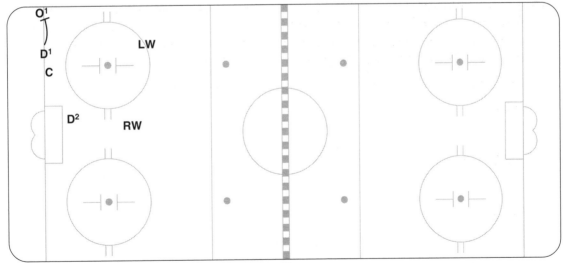

Figure 9.2   In the 2-3 system the two defensmen work with one forward to cover down low, while the wingers cover the slot and higher areas.

Playing Low Three on Three

D1, F1, and D2 work together and play the three low zones (hit zone, support zone, and net zone). The first forward back assumes the position of F1 (figure 9.3). Most of the time you want your center in this position

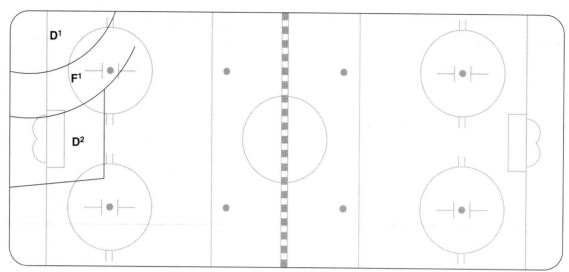

Figure 9.3   Low zone positioning for D1, F1, and D2.

(assuming he is the better of the three forwards in defensive play), so an exchange may be made when appropriate.

With the new interpretation of the rules at the NHL and amateur levels, body position means everything. Players are less able to create interference or hold up players, so early defensive positioning is critical.

Hit Zone

In this area, the first defensive player quickly closes on the puck carrier and makes contact with the opponent's body (figure 9.4). Show patience if the puck carrier has clear possession before you can get there. If you see the opposing player's number, then close quickly but be careful of hitting from behind; if you see the opposing player's logo, then contain. By containing the defensive player holds his position briefly then cautiously goes at the puck carrier. Containing means keeping he puck carrier in a set space by holding inside position and not letting him get to the net.

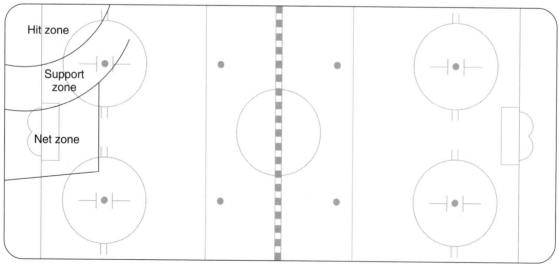

Figure 9.4   The hit zone, support zone, and net zone.

Once the puck is moved or he loses possession, stay with your check (do not hook) until that player is no longer a passing option. Now release that player and move into one of the other zones. The desired goal is for all defending players to keep their positioning between the opposing players and the goal you are defending.

Support Zone

In this zone (figure 9.4), the defensive player is aware of both the puck carrier and the closest passing option. Make sure the puck carrier cannot walk to the net if the first player gets beaten or falls down, and be ready to take away the opponent's closest passing option. Give yourself some space to react to the movement of players and the puck. At all times, try to stay above the goal line in support coverage. Because not many goals are scored by opposing teams from behind the goal line, your defensive positioning should not have you rushing into this area.

Net Zone

One player, usually a D, must always be in this zone (figure 9.4). Be aware of the third offensive player, and play halfway to any overload shooters (the offensive player on the half of the ice where the puck is). If there are any breakdowns, be patient and don't leave this area unless replaced by a teammate. Keep your stick on the ice. Stay out of the blue crease area, allowing the goaltender to have free movement.

Strong-Side Top Zone

F2 holds inside position at the top of the slot (figure 9.5). F2 must be ready to slide out tighter to his point if the puck carrier has the ability to pass there or cover him tight if he comes into the slot. When players cycle up high out of the corner, F2 must hold the top of the circle and deny inside access. Once a pass is made out to the point, F2 must approach the defenseman in the shooting lane so as to take away a direct shot on net.

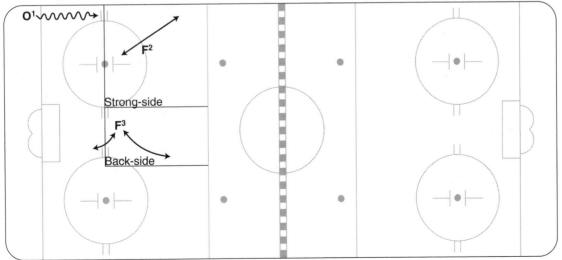

Figure 9.5   F2 covers the strong-side top zone, while F3 covers the back-side slot.

Back-Side Slot Coverage

F3 slides down lower on the back side (figure 9.5). If the net D is caught out of position, F3 will protect the low slot. Be aware of the back-side point sliding in. If F3 loses sight of where the backside defenseman is then he will have an opportunity to move into a dangerous scoring area for a wide pass outside the vision of the goaltender. F3 must always have his head on a swivel.

Low Zone Collapse

In this system, all five defensive players collapse in tight and basically play the opponent five on three low (figure 9.6). The theory is that you take away all plays to the slot by outnumbering the opponent and clogging up the scoring area. Most NHL teams use this collapse around the net style of play when the puck is below the goal line or after a point shot. Once the puck is passed back to the defenseman, the wingers who have collapsed in tight now move out to block the shooting lane.

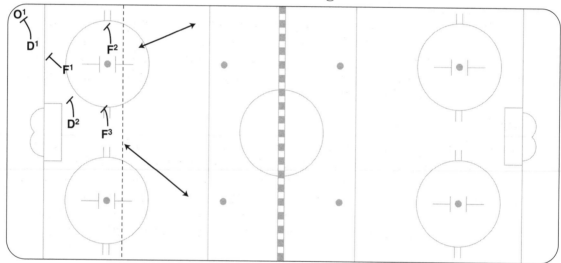

Figure 9.6   The low zone collapse coverage areas.

Playing Low Five on Three

D1, F1, and D2 work together and play the three low zones (hit zone, support zone, and net zone; figure 9.7). The first forward back assumes the position of F1. Most of the time you want your center in this position, so an exchange may be made when appropriate. The other two forwards sink in tight as well. The adjustment from the 2-3 system is that D2 can now move to the strong-side post F3 plays close to the net, covering the low slot while F2 (who is also collapsed below the dots) tries to deny passes back to the point.

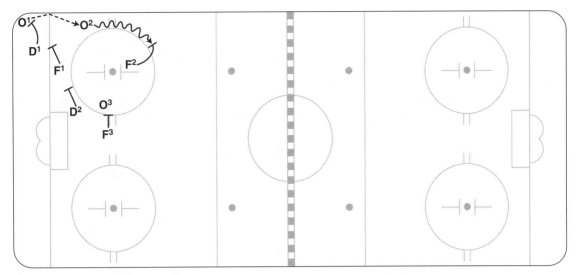

Figure 9.7   Low five on three coverage.

High Zone Coverage

When the offensive team moves the puck back to the point, F2 expands out in the shooting lane (figure 9.8). F2 should move quickly but be under control when the defenseman is ready to shoot. Get into the shooting lane when you anticipate a shot. At times it will be necessary to slide and block the shot. F3 holds the slot by moving out slightly and then when the opponent passes the puck D-D, F3 will move out in the shooting lane and F2 will rebound back to the low slot.

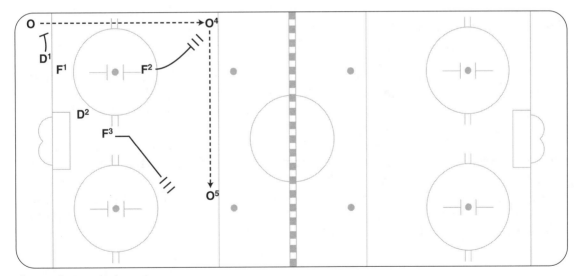

Figure 9.8   High zone coverage.

Half-Ice Overload

In this system, the defensive group basically splits the rink in half, trying to squeeze the offensive team to one half of the ice (figure 9.9). Plays to the back side are given up but made difficult because of the number of bodies in the way and how tough it is to make the long cross ice pass. D1, F1, and D2 take care of the strong-side corner and at times will be playing the opponent three on two in that area. These three defensive players squeeze the offensive space the opponents have to work in, and once the puck is recovered, they either quickly move it up the strong side or escape out the wide side.

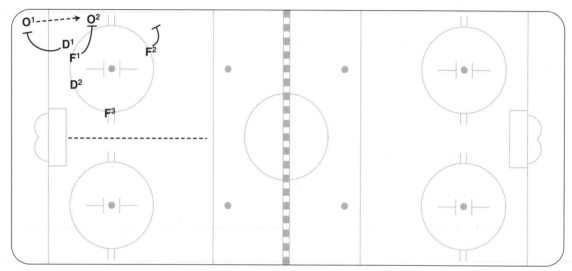

Figure 9.9   In the half-ice overload, the defensive team splits the rink in half.

If the defensive team has three players down in the corner, then the most important player off the puck is F3, who covers the slot but also shading to the strong side. F3 must be aware of the opponent's third forward and cover anyone who comes to the front of the net while at the same time be looking to see if the opposing back-side defenseman is moving into the scoring area. The opposition will try to sneak a defenseman down the back side, so F3 has to be aware and alert. F2 takes away the strong-side defenseman by playing much closer to the boards, therefore denying a pass out to the strong-side point. F2 needs to start inside the circle and then move out to cut off players cycling up the boards and having an active stick to cut off passes to the point.

The advantage of this system is that it is very difficult for the offensive team to find room to move and make plays on the strong side. A lot of teams like to cycle and then attack the net, but with this system, space to cycle is all but eliminated. When offensive players play against teams that use the half-ice overload, they often complain that they have no time! The one disadvantage is that quick plays to the net may result in a two on one on F3 if the opposing defensemen drives to the front of the net, but this is a difficult pass to make.

Man-on-Man Coverage

This system relies on constant puck pressure and denying time and space to the opponent. D1 starts by pressuring the puck carrier and then, after a pass is made, sticks with that player as he tries to get open. The only place D1 won't follow the player when he doesn't have the puck is out to the blue line; D1 has tight coverage on any players in the slot. F1 now pressures the pass and once again if the puck is moved sticks to his man (figure 9.10). This continues with D2 in the low zone area while F2 and F3 have responsibility for the opposing defensemen. F2 and F3 cover the defensemen whether they move in through the slot or slide down the boards. There is no confusion with the man-on-man system with regard to who a player is covering, but if the opposition is fairly creative and incorporates lots of motion, then it becomes harder to stay with your check. The new rules preventing clutching and grabbing have made it harder to play a true man-on-man system, but it can be very effective if the defenders are good skaters because the offensive team has minimal time with the puck before being pressured, and players away from the puck have trouble finding space to get open for a return pass.

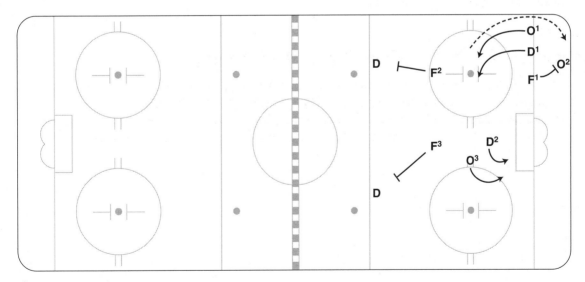

Figure 9.10   Man-on-man coverage.

Situational Guidelines for Defensive Zone Coverage

When covering active Ds, both F2 and F3 have a responsibility to cover their points if the opposing Ds move into scoring position. More and more teams are encouraging their defense to be active. If the defenseman they are covering moves into the slot, cover him tight. If the defenseman slides down the boards, there are two options. Either, cover tight, and move down the boards and into the corner with the D, or let D go and hold the inside position (figure 9.11). Once the opposing D is down low in the corner, he can be covered by your Ds or low forward. F2 or F3 can sink down and play inside but should not get dragged into covering a D in a non scoring area.

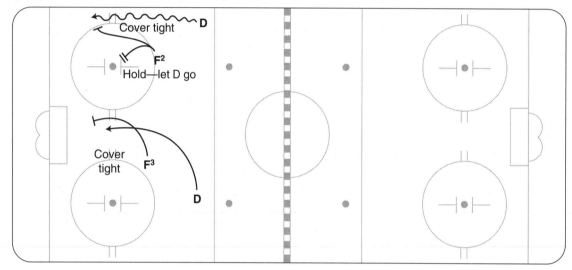

Figure 9.11   Covering active Ds.

Handling the Low Two on One Out of the Corner

Sometimes there is a breakdown, and the opponent attacks two on one versus the net defender (figure 9.12). Be patient and hold the net area. As the puck carrier advances, allow the goaltender to take one offensive player while holding the midnet position and defending the pass across.

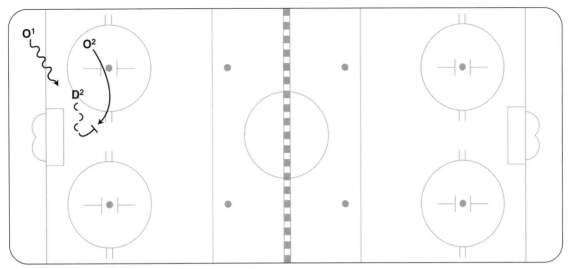

Figure 9.12   Handling a two on one out of the corner.

Defending a Player Behind the Net

First, recognize that there is a player behind the net and intercept the pass. If it is an even situation, pressure the puck carrier right away. When pressuring try to force the puck carrier away from where he got the pass and also away from support. If the player is unsure or the opponent has the advantage, wait to pressure until all defending players get back to position. RD flushes (for right-shot opponent); C holds mid-ice, aware of the back door; LD holds the back post; and the high wingers sink in tight (figure 9.13). Once the flush has started, LW (the side you are forcing them to) will start to slide back out toward his point, while RW stays tight in the slot. In all situations when the opposing team has the puck below the goal line, make sure only one defender is below the goal line so that the defenders outnumber the opponents in the house (or scoring area).

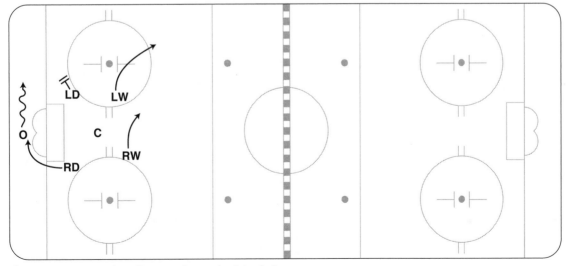

Figure 9.13   Defending a player behind the net.

Chapter 10
Penalty Kills

Today's game of hockey can be characterized by two focuses and two words: special teams. Over the past few seasons, all levels of hockey have endured much change. Most of this change stems from an increased attention by officials on the obstruction that had snuck into our game. Players and coaches had become very adept at running interference and slowing down not only the game but also its most skilled players. A by-product of this change is a gigantic increase in the volume of penalties and an obvious impact that power plays and penalty kills have on the outcome of each game.

The penalty kill has in many ways turned into an art. Players who in years past may have played a lesser role because of their lack of offensive gifts are now playing a major role making sure that the opposing power play does not affect their team's chances of winning. Here are the keys to successful penalty killing:

- **Outwork the power play.** Most PP units will relax to a degree because of the extra man, so be prepared to significantly outwork them.

- **Win face-offs.** Possession of the puck and a quick clear will not only force the PP unit to go back 200 feet (61 m) for the puck but will also frustrate the PP unit, which is what you want.

- **Talk.** Communication improves positioning and awareness.

- **No big hits.** Never hit on the PK, as tempting as it is; you should only "bump and run." It is a priority to keep your feet moving and pressure the opponent. Making a big hit takes players out of the play which you can't afford when already down one player.

- **Have an active stick.** Keep it on the ice at all times and in the right passing lane.

○ **Get body position in shooting lanes,** and know when to go down to block shots. Blocking shots can be a big boost to the penalty kill.

○ **When in the zone, pressure the puck in straight lines**—rebound back into position quickly after you pressure, and lead with your stick as you return.

○ **Compete hard for loose pucks.**

○ **When clearing the puck, make sure it goes 200 feet** (61 m). Try to score only when you have a lane to take the puck into the offensive zone.

○ **Never get tied up with the player at the net.** Most leagues prevent you from moving that player legally, so once he is there, do not create a double screen in front of your goaltender; play around him and have an active stick.

○ **Players coming out of the penalty box must know where to go.** Coaches should set rules for all players coming out of the box when the puck is in your end.

Face-Offs and Penalty Kills

Every penalty kill has one thing in common: It starts with a face-off. Many pundits of our game see the neutral zone face-off as a throwaway item, especially while killing penalties. We very much disagree. Every face-off is an opportunity to gain puck possession, and every detail of winning these face-offs must be attended to. For example, lazy positioning can seep into our game. Sometimes in the neutral zone both defensemen pull off the line and hang back toward their own end at face-offs.

In this simple example of attention to details, any time the left or right side of the face-off is left abandoned, it increases the opponent's ability to gain puck possession. Always place players on the penalty kill, including defensemen, tight to the face-off (figure 10.1), giving them an ability to contest for the loose puck and therefore increasing your ability to gain possession. Possession of the puck on the penalty kill may mean only seconds, but every second decreases your opponent's ability to score with the player advantage.

For obvious reasons, the defensive zone face-off becomes a very important component of a successful penalty kill. Proper possession of the puck in the defensive zone often allows your team to relieve pressure and advance the puck 180 feet (55 m) away from your goal.

A key component of aligning or positioning your players (especially who takes the face-off) has much to do with the center's strong side. During my nine seasons with the Montreal Canadiens, I played a number of those seasons with Guy Carbonneau. Carbo was a right shot, I was a left shot, and both of us were good at winning face-offs on our strong side. What an advantage! On face-offs to the left of our goalie, I could easily draw the puck on my backhand; face-offs to the right of our goalie put Guy on his backhand strong side.

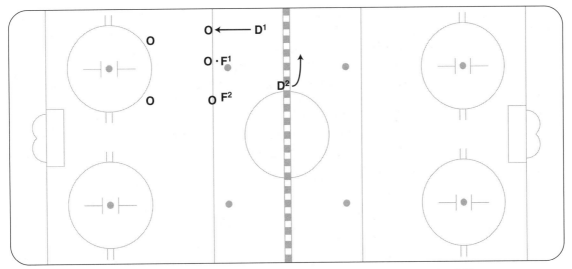

Figure 10.1   Always place players tight to the face-off on the penalty kill.

The defensive zone penalty-killing face-off alignment has many options. Let's discuss a few.

Most NHL teams try to have the center draw the puck back toward the corner, hoping that the boards-side defenseman can jump quickly off the line to gain possession of the puck or bump the puck to his partner behind the net (figure 10.2). It helps to have this boards-side defenseman on his forehand when he approaches the puck. If this is the case, the best option is to lay the puck to the inside winger, who moves quickly toward either the opposite half boards or the opposite side of the net.

On seeing the puck won cleanly, the inside winger races to the corner or the half boards to retrieve a bank pass or slow rim by the boards-side defenseman.

We have found over the years that minor details are very important, such as making sure a right-handed defenseman is on the ice to maximize

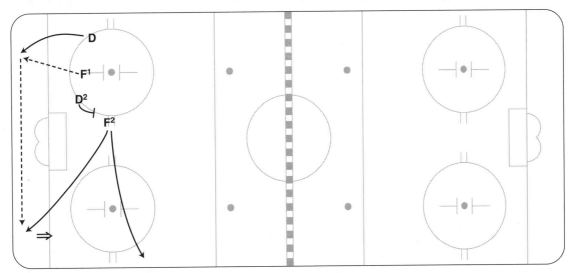

Figure 10.2   A common penalty kill face-off strategy is to have the center draw the puck back toward the corner.

a won face-off opportunity. (In this case, because the face-off is left of the net, it is advantageous to have a defenseman with a right-hand shot on the boards to best handle the puck if the draw is won cleanly.)

Never give your opponent soft possession of the puck off the draw. Always make sure that all opposing players are contested for possession of the puck (figure 10.3). Always make sure that if the puck is drawn to the boards that your team does not easily give up possession of the puck. Make sure the boards-side D contests any tied draws hard. You may say that these are small details, but *details* becomes an important word when dealing with the penalty kill.

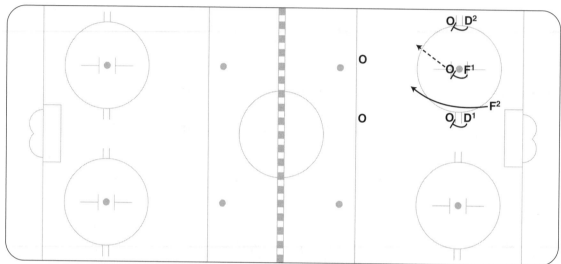

Figure 10.3   Always contest all opposing players off the draw.

There are some other important points to consider in regard to defensive zone PK face-off alignments. We prefer the winger to be inside the pocket of your team's inside defenseman (figure 10.4), and here's why. Hundreds of times we have seen this winger jump through toward the center, win a loose puck, and clear it down the ice.

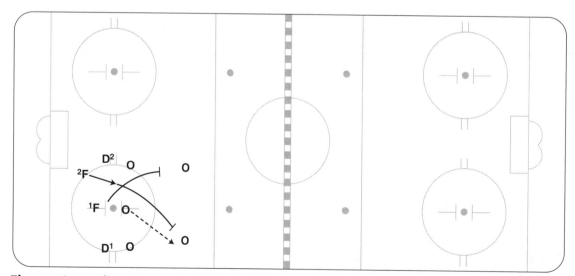

Figure 10.4   The winger should be inside the pocket of your team's inside defenseman.

We also prefer this alignment because the inside winger has a better chance to "jump" off the lost face-off and force pressure than the center does. In Montreal off a lost face-off, that inside winger would press the puck hard, and then the center would respond to the secondary positioning (figure 10.5). This works especially well now because face-off interference is called much more tightly. The opposition cannot obstruct this inside winger as much as in previous eras of our game.

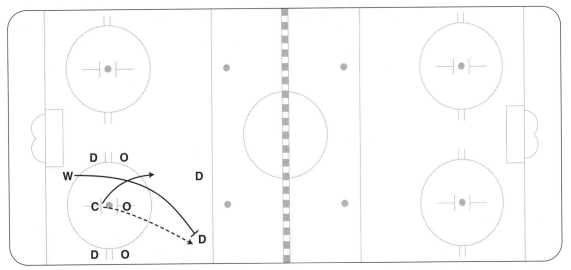

Figure 10.5   Off a lost face-off, the inside winger can press the puck hard with the center responding to the secondary positioning.

With the game tightening up, the obstruction rule has changed how teams set up their players for face-offs. In this alignment in the past, when the center cleanly won the face-off, the boards-side defenseman would hold up the opposing player a bit, the inside winger would hold up the opposing winger a bit, and the inside defenseman would retreat and slap the puck down the ice (figure 10.6). Obviously, this is still an excellent alignment, but both the winger and the boards-side D must be careful on the holdups.

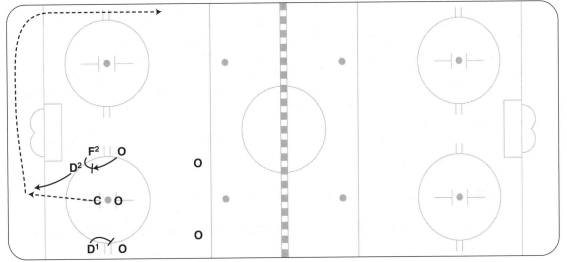

Figure 10.6   The inside D retreats and slaps the puck down the ice.

Another effective way to clear the defensive zone when the face-off is won cleanly is the winger press. In this alignment, the boards-side D rims the puck hard around the boards, and the winger now staying outside presses or runs the opposing D to make sure the puck departs the zone (figure 10.7).

Whatever face-off alignment is utilized, coaches can see how important it is to have every player on the ice in-sync and understanding their roles. Remember, the face-off is the only time that hockey players get to play football. Face-offs are a great opportunity for you or your center to call the play and then celebrate when the players on the ice perfectly execute it.

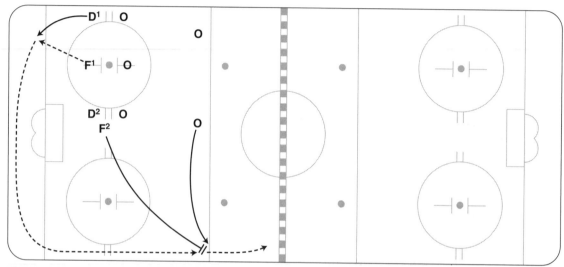

Figure 10.7 The boards-side D rims the puck hard around the boards.

Forechecking and Penalty Kills

Now that you have cleared the puck 200 feet (55 m) from your net (initiating the forecheck) with the help of your expert face-off alignment, let's look at ways to respond to your opponent's breakout. Many coaches prefer different styles of up-ice positioning, and it all depends on the objective of your attack. For example, do you want to angle your opponent toward the red line? Do you want to take away speed and a primary passing option? Do you want to pressure deep up ice or meet the attack at the far blue line? Do you want to prevent a long pass and possible breakaway? Your team's objective determines how your players, especially the two forwards, align themselves on the forecheck.

After clearing the puck or carrying it out of the defensive zone, penalty killers have three options:

1. Change to get fresh players on the ice. A change is the priority at any time close to 30 seconds into the shift.

2. Pressure the puck when it is dumped down, and try to disrupt the breakout.

3. Challenge the PP and try to score. Many PP units have a forward on defense and are made up of the team's best offensive players. On most teams these players lack defensive skills, so the PP unit's ability to defend is below average. If attempting to score, don't get fancy—take the puck straight to the net. If you try to make too many plays, there is a better chance of a turnover and most likely you will be caught and too tired to react appropriately. If you simplify the attack and go hard to the net, more than likely you will draw a penalty or get a decent scoring chance.

This section describes five forechecking options. In reality, the PK unit rarely disrupts the PP breakout deep in the opposition's own end; therefore, it is important on the forecheck to position yourself through the neutral zone so that you are able to pressure the entry.

Tandem Pressure is a more aggressive style of forecheck pressure allowing the forwards freedom to angle and press the puck carrier. This style puts more pressure on the opponent in the neutral zone but can spread out the 4 penalty killers over two zones.

The Forwards Wide approach offers token pressure up ice and creates 4 player alignment across the defending blue line. This forces the opposition to chip or dump the puck into the zone and accomplishes its goal of "taking the puck out of the power plays hands" where the PK now has an equal chance of retrieving the puck. The Forwards Wide approach works well against power plays who prefer to carry the puck into the zone on entries because pressure can be applied on that puck carrier to turn over the puck.

The Retreating Box (or the Backing-up Box) keeps all puck possession to the outside and allows angled pressure and no cross ice passing. The Retreating Box works well against power plays who prefer to dump the puck into the zone because it keeps the PK D further back into the zone and therefore gives them a better chance at puck retrieval. The Retreating Box does allow the power play more possession entries but never through the middle. In other words opponents can skate with speed on the outside of the box and maintain possession of the puck until challenged deeper in the zone.

The Same-Side Press forecheck forces the opponents entry towards one side of the ice where all the defending pressure can be applied. This system allows both forwards to angle the direction of the play and allows that strong side defenseman to step up and make the blue line hard to enter. Teams who move the puck well laterally in the neutral zone may have a chance to break this forecheck but the Same-Side Press makes it difficult to enter on the strong-side.

The Passive 1-3 backs up in unison and tries to hold a close gap in the neutral zone. This formation is more passive but has the same goal of getting the power play to dump the puck into the zone (taking the puck out of their hands) and giving the 4 penalty killers an opportunity to retrieve and ice the puck. This alignment is primarily set up to confront the PP unit at the blueline and force a turnover or dump in.

■ TANDEM PRESSURE

F1 angles and pressures the opposition, trying to get there as soon as the opposing player picks up the puck (figure 10.8). F1 recovers after forcing a pass or stays in the battle if he creates a scramble. F2 angles in on the first pass, making sure he is in position to get back while trying to force the player to unload the puck. D1 and D2 maintain a tight gap, making sure they are aware of any stretch players. F1 fills in the mid-ice lane, while F2 stays up in the middle, skating backward or angling forward and trying to force the entry to one side.

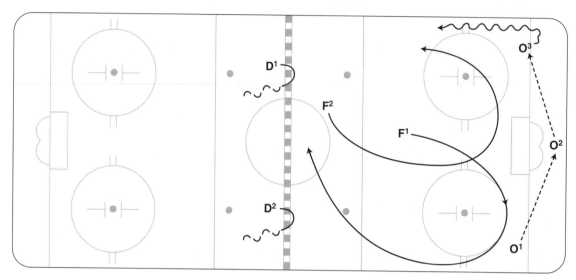

Figure 10.8

■ FORWARDS WIDE

F1 angles and pressures the opposition, trying to get there as soon as the opposing player picks up the puck (figure 10.9). F1 then moves back and takes the wide lane while skating forward. F2 swings and takes the opposite wide lane, also skating forward. D1 and D2 stay up in the middle; they need to have a tight gap and confidence to be tight in the neutral zone.

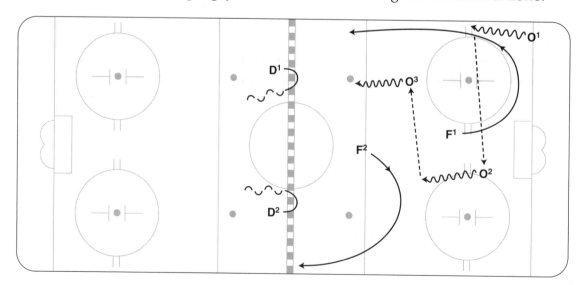

Figure 10.9

■ RETREATING BOX

F1 forces the opposition if he can and then skates backward up one side of the ice in line with the dots (figure 10.10). F2 skates backward up the other side. D1 and D2 tighten up in mid-ice. All four players skate backward together. Once the opposing puck carrier crosses the blue line, F1 or F2 forces that player to his backhand. Therefore, if the player is a left shot, then F2 forces him toward F1. F1 tries to deny the pass back to where he came from.

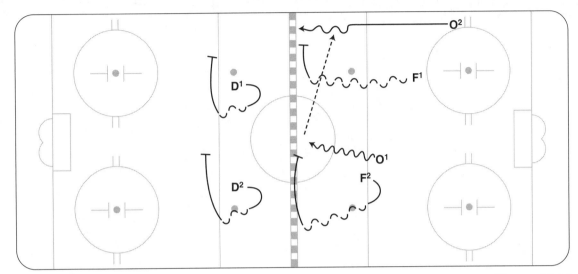

Figure 10.10

■ SAME-SIDE PRESS

F1 and F2 wait in the neutral zone for the opposition to break out (figure 10.11). F1 angles the puck carrier to one side with a good stick, preventing passes back. F2 angles across to the same side and goes after the pass or the puck carrier. D1 and D2 tighten up in mid-ice. D2 is ready to challenge passes to the far side, and D1 is ready to retrieve pucks dumped in.

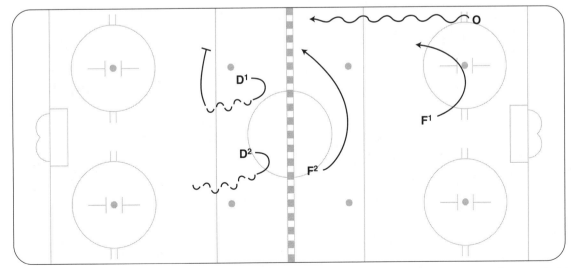

Figure 10.11

■ PASSIVE 1-3

F1 applies pressure only when he is sure he can get the puck and clear it or can force the other player as he picks up the puck (figure 10.12). F1 now retreats with a tight gap, initially skating backward and then forces the puck carrier to one side. F2 stays in mid-ice behind F1, also skating backward with a tight gap. D1 and D2 stay up; they need to have a tight gap and confidence to be tight in the neutral zone. They also must be aware of any stretch players getting behind them. D1 or D2 must attempt to confront the entry at the blueline by standing up the puck carrier and forcing a dump in.

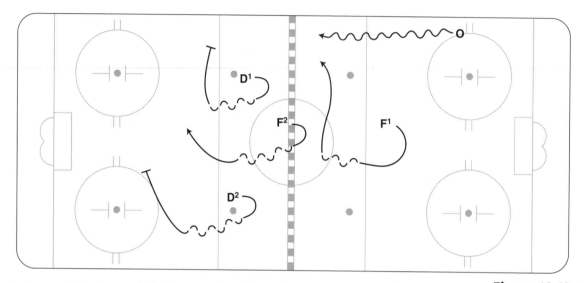

Figure 10.12

Pressuring the Entry

The entry is one area of the penalty kill where you should focus your time as you develop the special teams unit. If you stall the PP—at your blue line or as soon as they enter your zone—and clear the puck, you have effectively killed about 20 seconds off the clock and have a chance to change, while the PP unit will generally stay out and try to enter again. Teams may challenge the entry by making an immediate stand at the blue line, forcing the puck carrier at the half boards, or pressuring the dump-in. Described here are ways to confront the setup of the PP unit, depending on the forecheck used.

■ TANDEM PRESSURE

D1 confronts the puck carrier, at the blue line if possible, while F1 goes after any pucks chipped in (figure 10.13). F2 holds the slot. D2 retreats to the net or as an option for F1 to bump the puck to. If the PP unit carries the puck deeper, then D1 confronts the puck carrier at the half boards, and F1 seals up top. F2 holds the slot area and D2 the net area. If the puck is dumped in, then D2 goes hard to the dump-in. F1 and D1 also go to the puck. F2 holds the slot area.

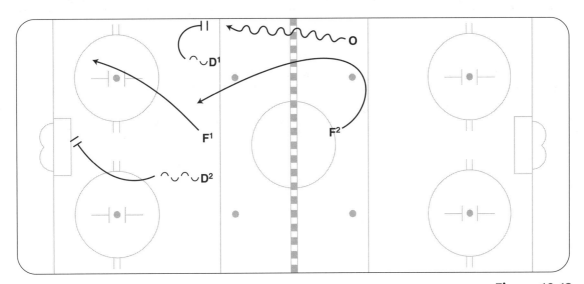

Figure 10.13

■ FORWARDS WIDE

D1 and D2 stay up in the middle where the PP unit will try to bring the puck (figure 10.14). If the pass is made to the wide lane, then F1 and F2 challenge the outside lanes. On the dump-in, F2 and D2 go to the corner along with D1. F1 supports the net.

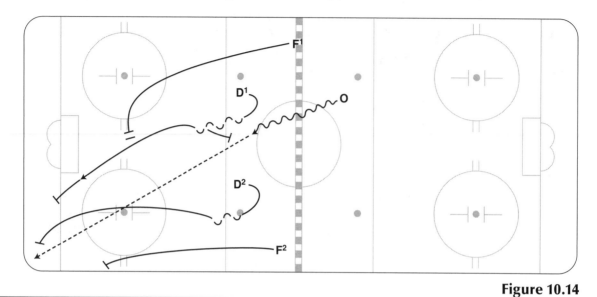

Figure 10.14

■ RETREATING BOX

F2 or D1 tries to confront the entry at the blue line (figure 10.15). D2 goes after pucks chipped in, and F1 holds mid-ice. If the PP unit skates the puck in, then D1 or D2 confronts the entry at the half boards. F1 and F2 hold the top positions. If the PP unit dumps the puck in, then D1 and D2 both go to the puck. The closest forward tightens up, and the other forward holds the slot.

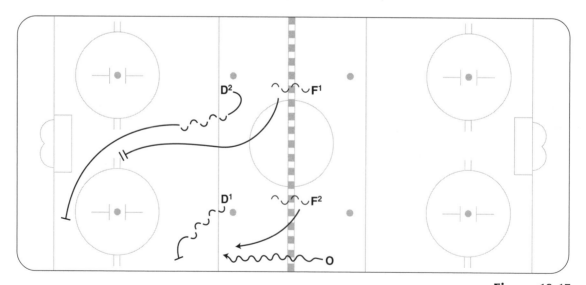

Figure 10.15

■ SAME-SIDE PRESS

F1 angles the puck carrier to the outside (figure 10.16). F2 tries to force the entry at the blue line or force the puck carrier to dump the puck. D2 goes after any pucks chipped in. With pressure from F1, F2, and D2, the PP usually cannot skate the puck in unless a pass is made to the wide side. On dump-ins, D1 goes to the corner with support from F1 and D2. F2 holds the slot.

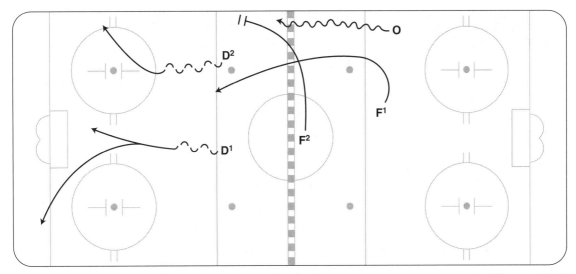

Figure 10.16

■ PASSIVE 1-3

This is a similar setup to the tandem press. D1 confronts the puck carrier at the blue line if possible, while F2 goes after any pucks chipped in (figure 10.17). F1 holds the slot. D2 retreats to the net or as an option for F2 to bump the puck to. If the PP unit carries the puck deeper, then D1 confronts the puck carrier at the half boards and F1 seals up top. F2 holds the slot area and D2 the net area. If the puck is dumped in, then D2 goes hard to the dump-in. F2 and D1 also go to the puck. F1 holds the slot area.

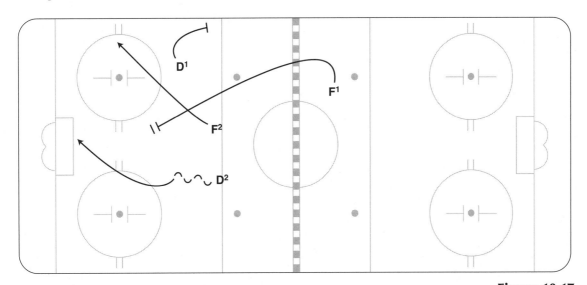

Figure 10.17

Defensive Zone Play

While in the defensive zone, the penalty-killing unit moves from "active contain" to "contain pressure" to "all-out pressure." This is based on the reads of when to pressure. Every coach will have a varying degree of pressure he is comfortable with. Some coaches make a simple rule for their players to read when to press and when not to press. The rule is called "eyes" and "backsides." If your player sees that the opposing player with the puck is looking directly at them they move into a more passive "containing" mode. If the player see an opponent's "backside or number" then they apply maximum pressure. Obviously when a player is turned to get the puck and not facing mid-ice (backside and numbers) he is not ready to make a play and therefore can be pressured harder. Remember, once one player moves to pressure, each subsequent pass must be pressured. The penalty killers should assert more pressure when they know the puck carrier will have a difficult time controlling the puck and making a good play. Here are some examples:

○ the PP has poor control or a player juggles a pass,

○ the player with the puck has no immediate support,

○ the player with the puck has his back turned to the net,

○ the puck is being rimmed from one player to another along the boards,

○ there is a loose puck from a rebound or missed shot, or

○ the ice conditions are poor late in the period.

Following are some situations PK units may face and how to play them. We describe different power play options and how the penalty killers should react.

■ LOW–HIGH PRESS

When O2 receives a pass from O4 or O1, D1 pressures him up the boards (figure 10.18). D2 is ready to take away any return passes to O1. F1 takes away the passing lane to O4. F2 stays in the slot, aware of passing options to the back side. Players should keep their sticks in the most dangerous passing lane which could be to the slot player or backside D.

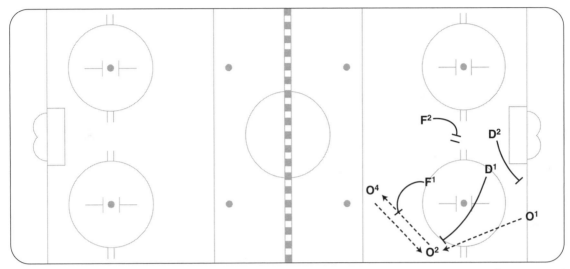

Figure 10.18

■ CZECH PRESS

F1 forces O4 at the point (figure 10.19). O4 passes back to O2 on the side boards but too high for D1 to pressure. F1 now pressures back on the pass and forces O2 down the boards. D1 is ready to pressure the pass to O1. D2 holds the slot and prevents any cross-ice passes. If the puck is passed back to O4, there are two options: (1) F1 can return up high to pressure, or (2) F2 can pressure and F1 returns to the slot. F2 would only pressure if he can get there at the same time as the pass.

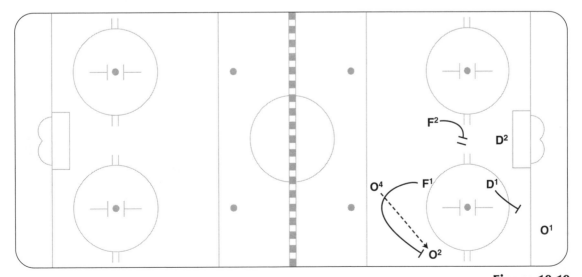

Figure 10.19

■ DIAMOND FORCE

F1 pressures or stays in O4's shooting lane as he slides with the puck across the blue line (figure 10.20). D1 moves up slightly, ready to go after O2 if the pass goes there. F2 sinks back into the diamond and is ready to get in the shooting lane of passes to O5. D2 plays the net. Stay in this formation as long as O4 continues to stay in the middle of the blue line.

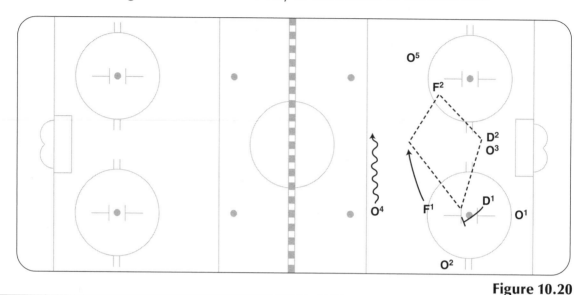

Figure 10.20

■ FORCING THE BACK OF THE NET

Many teams like to set up behind the net on the PP or take the puck behind. D1 recognizes a chance to pressure and forces O1. D2 holds normal position, avoiding screens or picks and is ready to challenge the walkout (figure 10.21). F1 slides down to replace D1. F2 moves to the middle of the triangle in front of the net, aware of any opposing Ds coming in from the point. It is also important to try to deny passes to players behind the net—anticipate that play, and cut it off as the pass is made.

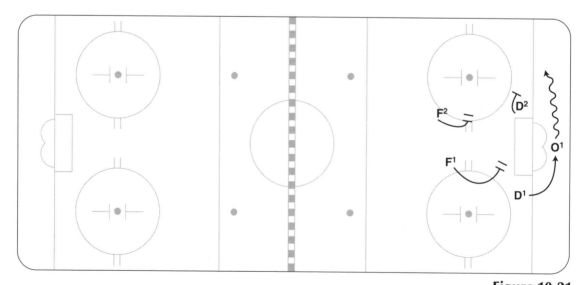

Figure 10.21

■ TIGHT COLLAPSE

If the puck does end up behind your net, then all players should sink in tight (figure 10.22). Be aware of players moving in, and have an active stick to take away passing lanes as the puck carrier moves out. D1 or D2 may hold their position or force the puck carrier to one side.

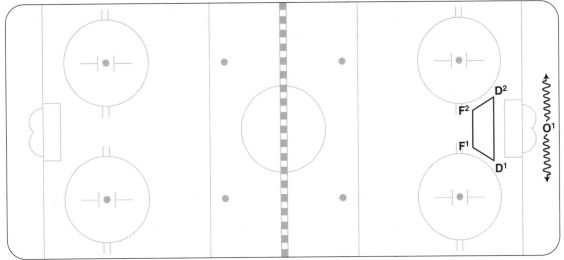

Figure 10.22

Three-on-Five Penalty Kill

The three-on-five penalty kill is a difficult challenge but at its best can also be a work of art. The three on five is one area of the team game that, when successful, can create excitement and positive bench momentum for your team. The key to defending the three on five is to have all three players totally in sync with each other's movements and the system that you implement. Coaches have to decide how tight they want to play it or how aggressive they are going to get. Following are three approaches that different coaches like to use.

■ INVERTED TRIANGLE

This setup is suited to kill a five on three where the opponent has two Ds up top (figure 10.23). F1 and D1 (D1 could be a defenseman, although some teams like to use another forward) move up and down on their sides as the puck is moved from high to low. F1 and D1 should not go too wide or too high. D2 plays the net area and moves from post to post. D2 must deny the side-to-side pass from O1 to O2. F1 and D1 must be ready to block shots. During five on threes, it is key to stay tight and compact and be strong on rebounds.

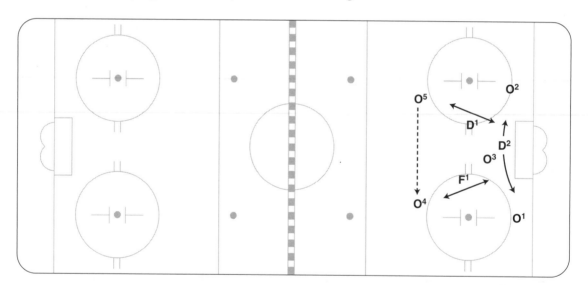

Figure 10.23

■ SPLIT THE D'S

This set up is another option to kill a five on three penalty where the opponent has two D up top (figure 10.24). F1 stays in the middle of the ice denying any high passes through the middle and any passes between the two D. D1 and D2 play the base of the triangle. When the puck is at the bottom with O1 then D1 forces him out wide and D2 covers the net. F1 stays in the low slot. This penalty-kill setup does not give up much down low while also taking away any D-D up high passes with the stick of F1.

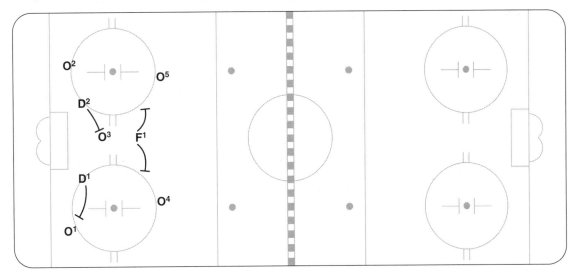

Figure 10.24

■ TRIANGLE, ONE HIGH

This setup is primarily suited to kill a five on three where the opponent has one D up top. F1 stays in the middle of the ice (figure 10.25). When the puck is up top, he stays head to head with the one opposing D. D1 and D2 form the base of the triangle. When the puck is at the bottom with O1, then D1 forces him out wide and D2 covers the net. D1 and D2 must also get in the shooting lanes of O3 and O4 when they have the puck. F1 stays in the low slot. Recognize where one-timer shots could come from, and have an active stick.

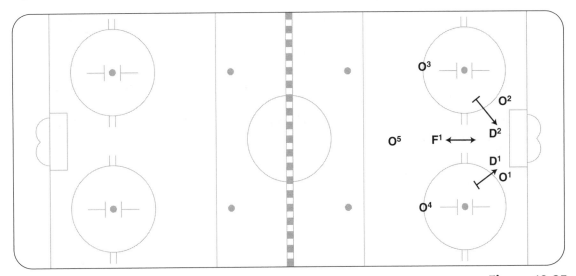

Figure 10.25

Three-on-Four Penalty Kill

The three-on-four penalty kill adds its own complexity and is similar to yet different from killing the three on five. The difference is that the defending three must decide if they are going to take away the top two shooters or stay near the front of the net. Usually the 4on3 is much easier to kill than the five on three. The PK unit focuses on playing around the man at the net leaving them three on three against the shooters.

■ TRIANGLE, ONE HIGH

Most teams on a four-on-three power play will set up in a diamond with one player at the net, so the triangle penalty kill with one high is the most effective system to use. F1 stays in the middle of the ice (figure 10.26). When the puck is up top, he stays head to head with the one opposing D. When the puck is passed, F1 stays in the middle and uses his stick to deny the pass from O2 to O3. D1 and D2 are ready to move out and take the shooting lane away from O2 and O3. D1 and D2 do not tie up with O1 at the net but are ready to defend his stick and get body position if the puck is shot through.

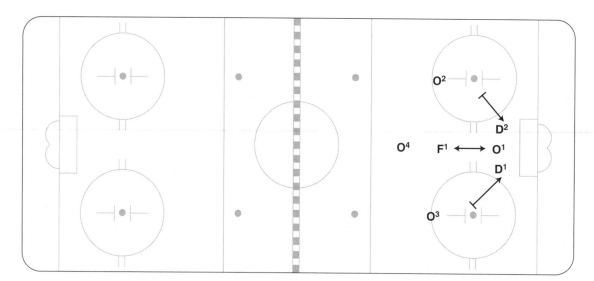

Figure 10.26

Remember the old adage that "defense wins championships." Working on your teams PK structure, getting all players on the same page and having your goaltender be your best penalty killer are all ways to give your team a better chance to win.

Part III

Special Game Situations

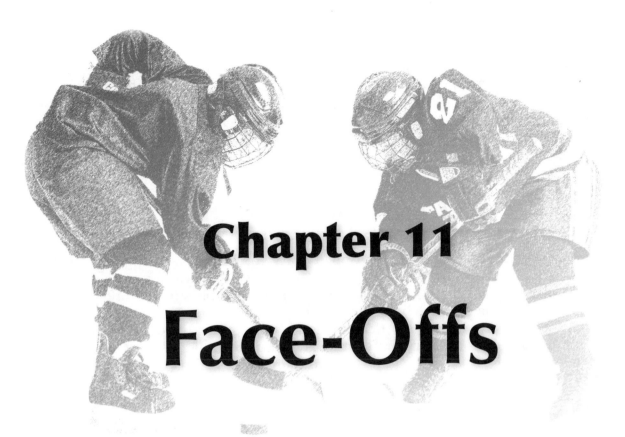

Chapter 11

Face-Offs

The offensive face-off gives coaching staffs and players time to implement set plays, making it the only time that hockey players get to play football. Teams should prepare for face-offs in a number of ways. First, practice them by going through the plays on a walk-through basis. Once a month, take time in practice to run through what you want the players to do at each face-off dot. It does take time, and it tends to slow the pace of practice, but there are roughly 60 face-offs in a game, which means 60 times to win or lose possession of the puck—so it is worth the time. In addition to all players going through the face-offs, the centers must work on the skill of taking the draw. It doesn't take long for a coach to quickly do 50 reps with a center before or after practice, focusing on his technique. Centers should work on winning draws on the forehand, on the backhand, by tying up, and at times by touching the puck through to catch the opposition by surprise.

Consider having a face-off play book that includes responsibilities as well as diagrams illustrating the execution patterns. Some teams have developed a DVD to give to the centers, who much like a quarterback in football need to know the formation and how to set up. This DVD should have dialogue and a clear illustration of the plays. Because of the clarity and camera angle, it may be best to collect plays from NHL, college, and junior games and then edit the material down for the players.

Finally, depending on the age of your group, you may want to have the centers pick the option for their line for that night or come to you with a play they think will work. This type of player ownership can be effective; the players will definitely focus if it is their play because they want it to work.

Have face-off plays for all face-off dots and for specific game situations. The way a team lines up five on five is much different from four-on-four and three-on-three situations. Don't forget power-play five on four, four on three, and five on three; penalty-kill four on five, three on four, and three on five; and late-game pulled goaltender plays defensively and offensively. Over the course of my NHL career across three different teams and seven different head coaches, we implemented many face-off set plays, but they tended to be drawn from the following categories.

Offensive Zone Face-Offs

Offensive zone face-offs are an opportunity to create a scoring chance off a set play. Even if teams lose the draw there are ways to still recover possession and get a shot or chance. Many very sophisticated offensive face-off alignments have been developed over the years, but these alignments cover the basics of offensive zone strategy and provide enough options for teams at every level. You may want to challenge your staff to come up with a set play of their own, but don't overwhelm your team with too many choices.

Offensive Zone: Won Draws

In the offensive zone, it is critical to win the draw and maintain possession. This section describes various set plays off won draws. A team cannot run all of them every night. It is important to have some variance but like all other systems of play, execution is the key to success. Give the team one play to run for every game and that way they will become used to all the set ups so that later in the year they can adjust on the spur of the moment. Also having variety in plays from game to game keeps the opposition off balance and forces them to have to react in coverage. Make the opposition coches work to figure out what you are running and how to cover that set up.

■ DEEP POSSESSION

For a number of reasons, an offensive center might call a face-off play where he actually helps his opponent win the face-off back toward the corner of the offensive zone (figure 11.1). The tactic behind this deceived loss is to have both wingers positioned and ready to press the defender when he wins the draw back to the corner. This quick and unexpected pressure often turns over the puck and therefore creates its desired effect, which is puck possession and a possible scoring chance or play on the net. Off the turnover, the player with the puck may decide to make a quick play to the net or take the puck behind the net and come out the other side. This strategy should be used only once or twice a game or if the center is struggling to win draws against a particular opponent (this gives that player a strategy to gain possession while losing the draw).

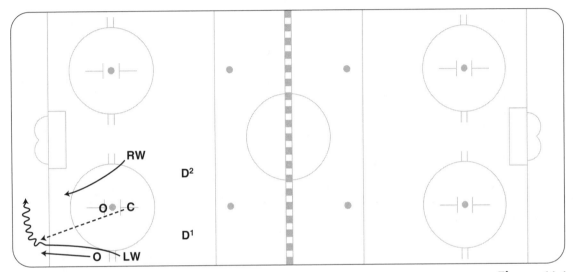

Figure 11.1

■ INSIDE WINGER DRAW

This face-off starts with the direct intent to win the face-off back to the offensive defenseman. As defending players scramble to front or block the shooting lane of the offensive defenseman, the inside winger RW skates above the circle and out to the side boards (figure 11.2). The center and LW must go hard to the net. The offensive defenseman's goal is to pull the puck toward the middle of the ice and fake a slapshot. As defenders react to this deception, the defenseman passes the puck laterally to the inside winger, who ends up with a clear shot toward the net through traffic. One variation is for C to drive the net and then push back to get open in the higher slot area. RW can now pass to C.

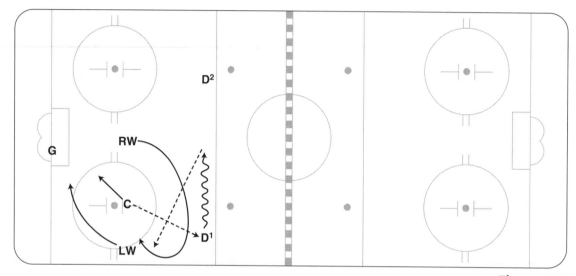

Figure 11.2

■ ROLL OUT

This offensive face-off alignment works well against teams who press hard towards both defensemen off the faceoff. As the two wingers press the D this Roll Out alignment gives a great pass and shot option. Off a won draw to D1, the two wingers (RW and LW) change positions (figure 11.3). The center drives to the front of the net. D2 drives wide; D1 backs across the the blue line, fakes a shot, and passes to LW, who has found the soft ice (high and lateral from D1). LW now has the option of shooting through traffic or passing to RW or D2.

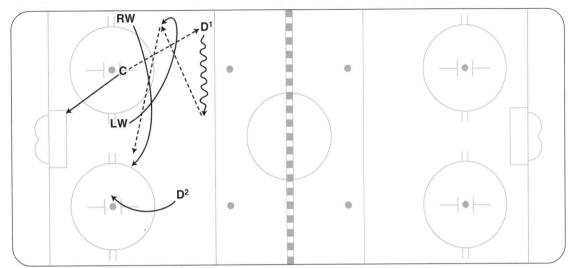

Figure 11.3

■ END AROUND

Much like the inside-out draw, this alignment uses the inside winger moving to the boards (figure 11.4). Instead of a high option, it creates an opportunity to take the puck to the net low. This face-off also starts with the direct intent to win the face-off back to the offensive defenseman, but the puck doesn't make it back and lies in the space right behind the center. The inside winger (RW) pulls or draws back toward the boards and in doing so grabs the puck and goes around the pile. As RW moves toward the back of the net, he may either take the puck to the net or pass to C or LW, who attempt to get open.

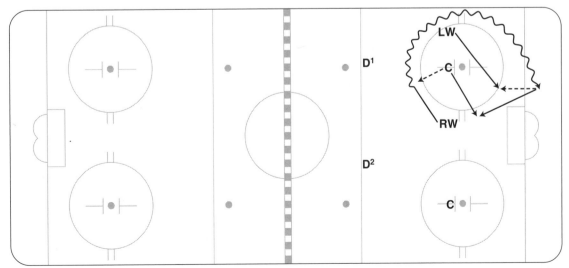

Figure 11.4

■ OFF-SIDE SHOT

Some face-offs are not always won directly or completely back to the point. When the center senses that he is going to tie-up the opponents stick and and win puck possession with his feet then this simple alignment is effective. In this face-off alignment, the two wingers typically switch positions, unless the boards-side winger is already shooting off his strong side. The center looks to win possession of the puck in the space just slightly behind him (figure 11.5). This allows the boards-side winger to step laterally toward the net and place a quick shot on net through traffic. Sometimes in this situation the center only has to tie up his opponent and leave the puck in the space behind him, which allows the winger to step into the shot.

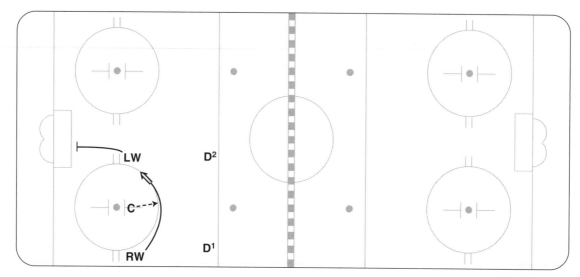

Figure 11.5

■ SAN JOSE SLIDE

This offensive face-off alignment works well when your team is trying to change things up and is another play that creates a lot of confusion for the defensive team. The center draws the puck back to D1, who moves quickly down the boards as he receives it (figure 11.6). The RW who is on the boards rolls over the top of the circle and sets up on the far post (the back door) taking the defender with him. The LW also goes to the net, giving the defenseman an option to pass to the net at any time. As D1 moves down the boards, C makes it look as if he is going to the net and then moves back a couple of steps into a soft area in the high slot and is open for a one-timer pass from D1. The reason C will be open is that the opposing center will probably go after D1. This movement off the face-off creates confusion in coverage for the defensive team.

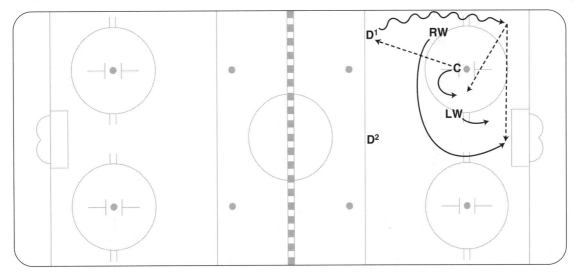

Figure 11.6

■ FOUR UP

There are times in the game when, like football with little time left on the clock, the team is looking for a simple Hail Mary type play. With a four-up face-off alignment, both wingers are on the inside and one D is down on the boards-side hash marks (figure 11.7). This alignment gives the center a lot of options, making it hard for the defending team to cover. Some defending teams will try to shoot the puck out past the one defenseman on the blue line; guard against that happening by having the inside winger slightly back and in the lane. The four-up face-off allows the center to tap the draw ahead and then pass to one of the two wingers in front; draw the puck back to D1 for a screen shot; or steer the puck to the boards for D2 to shoot or to pass to D1. This alignment is often used when there are seconds left on the clock at the end of periods or the end of games because it results in a quick play on net with numbers in front.

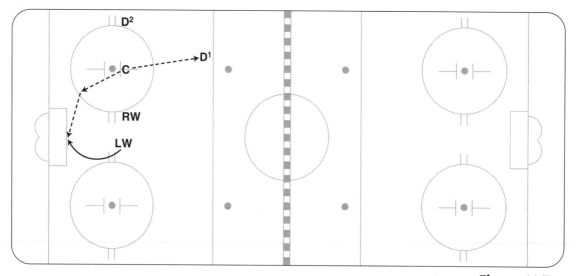

Figure 11.7

■ TIE-UP FOR POSSESSION

At times, centers just look to create possession of the puck for their team. Possession is often best obtained not by trying to win the puck but rather by blocking or tying up the stick of the opposing center (figure 11.8). If the offensive center can obstruct the stick of the defending center long enough, this allows both offensive wingers to attack the face-off circle to try to win puck possession. This strategy is often referred to as scrambling the puck. There are times in games when one center is dominating the other, so for the player who is constantly losing the draw, tying up the other center increases the odds of your team getting the puck.

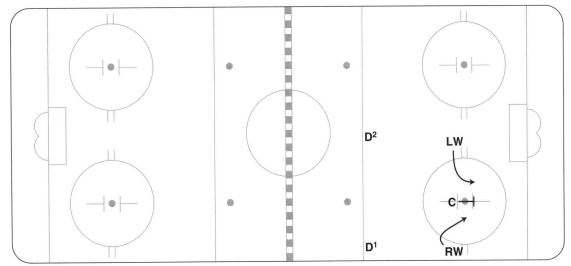

Figure 11.8

Offensive Zone: Lost Draws

Players should be prepared to win the draw and set up offensive plays as just described, but they should also know what to do when the center loses the draw. If players are ready to react and they understand how they are going to pressure the opposition to recover the puck, they will be much more successful in doing so. Listed here are strategies to regain possession and essentially initiate a forecheck.

■ DOUBLE PRESS

When the C loses the draw, he moves to a high position in the slot (figure 11.9). RW shoots through on the inside of the circle and pressures the defenseman getting the puck. RW must make sure the D doesn't turn quickly up the strong side. Force the defenseman to go into pressure by pushing him out the wide side. LW also jumps quickly to take away the wide side of the net and any D-to-D passes. D1 is ready to pinch on any pass to the opposing winger on the far boards. D2 stays in mid-ice as the safety

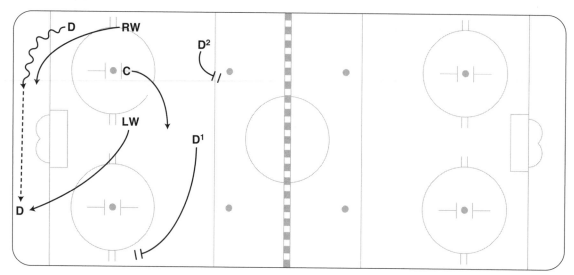

Figure 11.9

■ 1-2-2 FORCE

On the lost draw, RW pressures hard into the corner, forcing the defenseman around the net or to pass to his partner (figure 11.10). On any D-to-D passes, RW moves across either behind or in front of the net and forces. C is ready to take away plays up the right boards and takes away the mid-ice seam as the puck moves to the wide side. LW takes away the far boards. D1 and D2 stay in mid-ice and react to any passes up the middle.

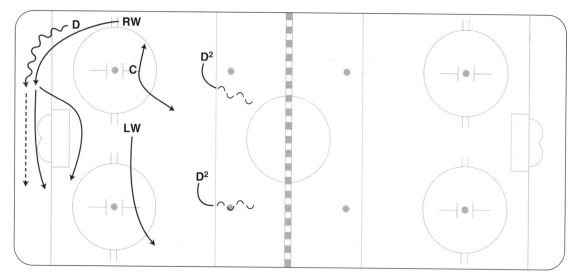

Figure 11.10

Neutral Zone Face-Offs

At one time, many coaches gave little thought to draws in the neutral zone, especially European coaches. Their feeling was that they were not important and didn't lead to anything. Most times their players would line up and halfheartedly take the draw. Now almost all coaches realize the importance of winning the face-off and gaining puck possession. As a result of the change in emphasis on neutral zone draws, many new strategies have evolved to create a quick attack off this face-off or to apply forechecking pressure when the draw is lost.

Neutral Zone: Won Draws

There are only a few face-off plays that create an offensive advantage in the neutral zone. Opponents will press with one or two players off a lost face off in the neutral zone, taking away passing lanes or closing ice, so having a plan with the puck is crucial. These actions tend to emulate neutral zone re-group options for moving the puck up ice. Described here are seven face-off plays from the center-ice and blue-line face-off dots.

■ CENTER ICE, THREE OPTIONS

C draws the puck back to D1, who passes to D2 (figure 11.11). C swings away and builds up speed. RW stretches to the far blue line. LW slants in to the middle of the blue line. D2 has the option to pass up to RW on the stretch, to LW in the mid-ice seam, or to C wide. D2 may also skate the puck to the red line and dump it in for C on the wide side.

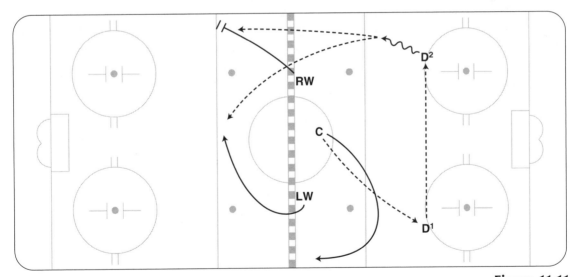

Figure 11.11

■ HIGH DEFLECTION

This face-off play also takes place at the center circle. Once C wins the draw, he moves above the red line (figure 11.12). Both wingers go out to the top corner of the blue line. D1 passes to D2, who looks to pass to C for a quick chip into the corner for RW. D1 may also pass to RW, who chips the puck behind the defense for C to pick up. This is a good play to start the game and apply quick forechecking pressure against the opponent.

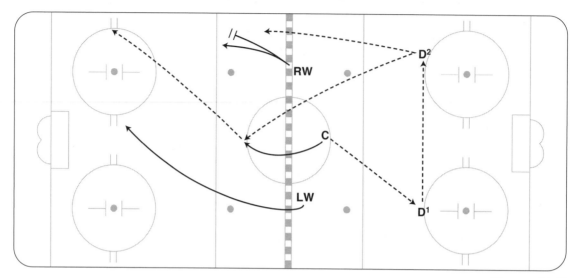

Figure 11.12

■ FORWARD BACK

LW drops back for the draw, with LD up (figure 11.13). C pushes the puck to the left side. Anticipating the draw, LW shoots through the hole and looks to skate or chip the puck by the opposing defenseman. RW also jumps quickly with LW.

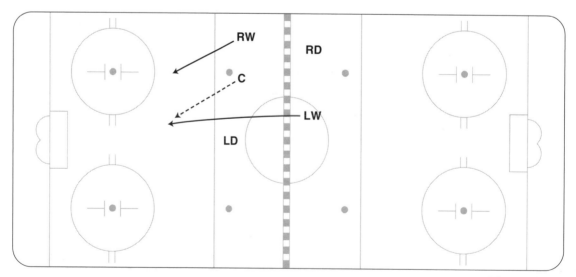

Figure 11.13

■ WEAK-SIDE SLANT

This face-off takes place at the defensive blue line. C draws the puck back to D1, who passes to D2 (figure 11.14). D2 skates to mid-ice. LW picks or screens the player inside so that D2 has more time with the puck. RW goes hard to the corner of the far blue line. D2 banks the puck to the high blue line area for RW to skate to. C jumps up through the middle to potentially create a two on one on the opposing defenseman.

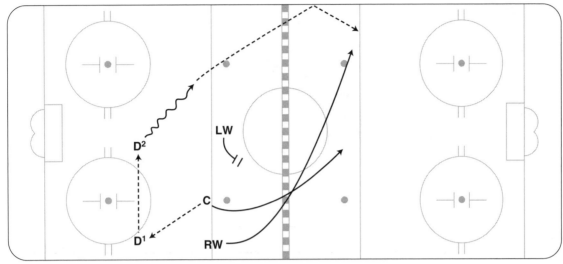

Figure 11.14

■ CENTER SLASH

C wins the puck back, and D2 passes to D1 (figure 11.15). RW reads clear possession and sprints to the far blue line. C blocks the opposing C and then sprints through the middle lane. LW stays wide and low for a cross-ice support pass. D2 drops to support D1. D1 has pass options to C or RW sprinting to the far blue line and, if neither is open, has the wide pass back to LW.

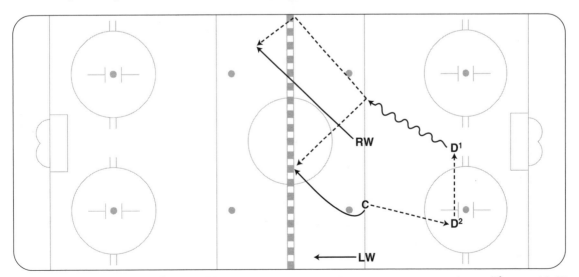

Figure 11.15

■ CENTER SWING-AWAY

Off a won draw, C swings away from the D-to-D pass (figure 11.16). LW sprints toward the boards, and RW fills the middle lane. D2 may pass to LW or RW, but the main option is to get the puck wide to C who has built up a lot of speed.

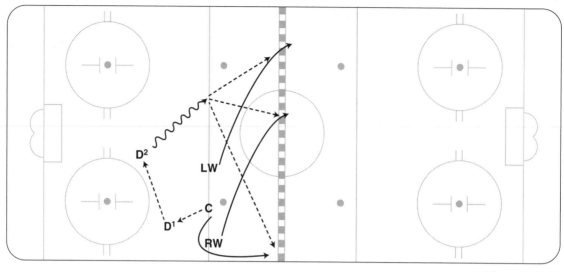

Figure 11.16

■ HARD RIM

This face-off is used in leagues with touch icing when the team desperately needs to get possession in the offensive zone and create a quick scoring chance. There is a risk of icing the puck. C draws the puck back to D1, who quickly shoots it hard along the boards into the far end (figure 11.17). LW races to the puck, trying to beat the opposing D. Once LW gets the puck, he bumps it behind the net to RW, who then looks to bring it to the net.

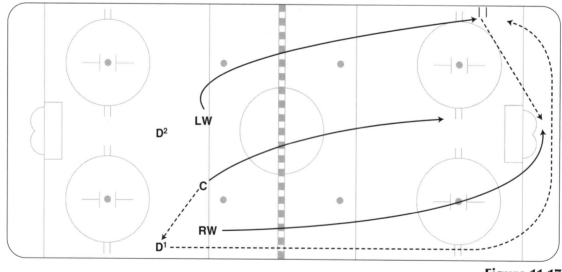

Figure 11.17

Neutral Zone: Lost Draws

To regain possession of the puck off a lost draw, these strategies may be used on any of the five neutral zone face-off circles. In most situations, this sets up a team's neutral zone forecheck.

■ DOUBLE PRESS

When the draw is lost, both wingers move quickly to pressure the opposing defense (figure 11.18). C locks the mid-ice area, preventing any passes to the other team's center. D1 and D2 are ready to take away passes up the boards and to move up quickly to pinch on the pass.

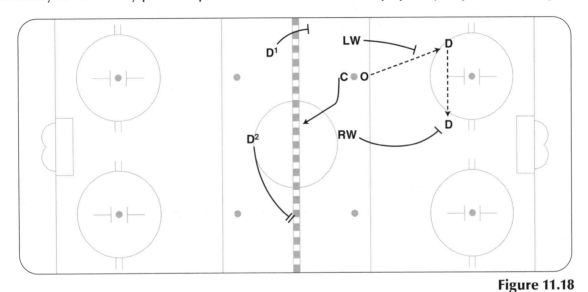

Figure 11.18

■ BOARD-SIDE PRESS

On the lost draw, the board-side winger (LW) forces the defense to pass the puck across the ice, into traffic (figure 11.19). C locks the middle. RW takes away the far boards. D1 and D2 keep a tight gap in mid-ice.

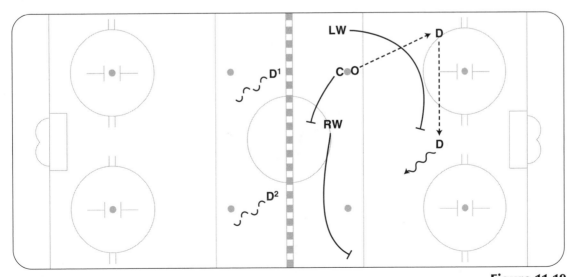

Figure 11.19

■ INSIDE-OUT PRESS

When the draw is lost, C quickly moves up between the two opposing defensemen and angles the puck carrier to the outside (figure 11.20). As C forces the play to the right, RW takes away the boards and any passes to that winger. LW locks the middle. D1 is ready to get any chip plays in behind RW. D2 plays mid-ice while being aware of passes to the wide side.

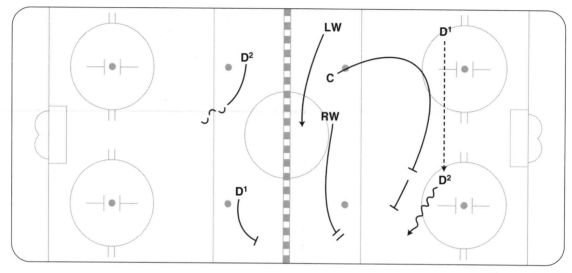

Figure 11.20

Defensive Zone Face-Offs

Winning a face-off in the defensive zone results in an opportunity to break the puck out and go on the attack. Losing the face-off in the defensive zone forces a team to defend and essentially go into defensive zone coverage until a turnover happens. We discuss both situations and provide strategies for each.

Defensive Zone: Won Draws

Described here are seven plays that teams can use when they win the draw in the defensive zone. Teams should practice breaking out on a won draw from both sides of the ice. The option used will depend to a degree on how the opposition forechecks and also what you are comfortable your team can execute. The final two options in this section, the breakaway and quick-change plays, are trick plays that might be used only a couple times a year. They can be used at any time of the game but generally are saved for moments when you are down by a goal, because there is a degree of risk in each of them. The rate of successfully completing these plays is much less than for the other provided, but if your opponents are not ready, you may catch them by surprise

■ SPIN AND UP STRONG-SIDE

If the opposition forechecks with their board side winger hard and also takes away the pass to D2 then D1 goes back for the puck and spins off pressure, moving the puck up to LW on the strong-side boards. Before reversing the puck or spinning off, D1 must first carry the pressure to make the opposition think he is going behind the net. C supports low, and RW moves across to support (figure 11.21). D1 may also bank the puck off the boards or glass into the neutral zone, and both wingers can race to that area. This will surprise teams who pinch their defense and may result in a two on one.

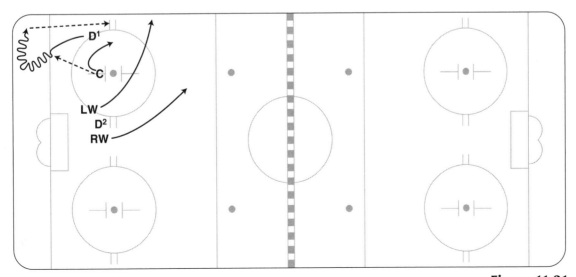

Figure 11.21

■ REVERSE TO CENTER

Once again the opposition team pressures hard with the boardside winger. D1 goes back for the puck and carries the pressure, trying to gain the back of the net. Knowing that he will not make it, he reverses the puck to C. Depending on pressure, D2 supports the front of the net or moves to the wide side, ready for a D-to-D pass. D2 should stay in front whenever D1 is under heavy pressure. LW moves back to support the boards, and RW moves across the ice in support (figure 11.22).

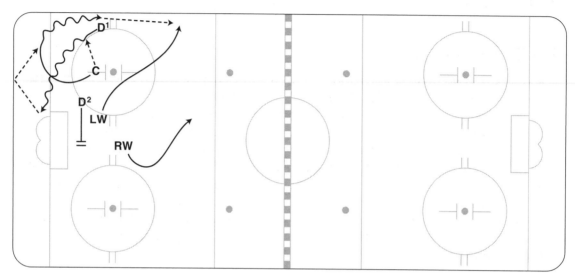

Figure 11.22

■ D-TO-D SHORT POST

Off a won draw, D1 gets the puck and makes a short pass to D2 at the near post (figure 11.23). From the near post, D2 skates behind the net and reads options to rim the puck, make a direct pass to the winger or center in mid-ice, or possibly execute a return pass to his partner.

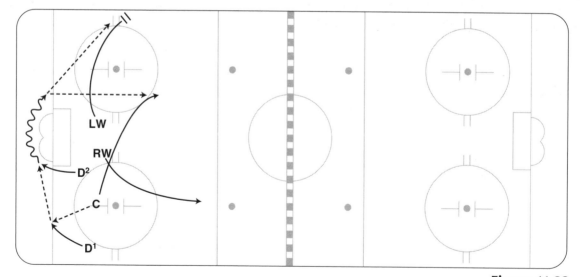

Figure 11.23

■ BUMP TO PARTNER

If the opposition only forechecks with one player, D1 quickly bumps the puck to D2 who releases to the wide side of the net in anticipation of the D-to-D pass. When D2 moves out to the wide side, he should try to be turned around facing up ice and ready for the pass when it arrives. RW moves out to the boards, and LW comes across through the high slot. C supports low (figure 11.24).

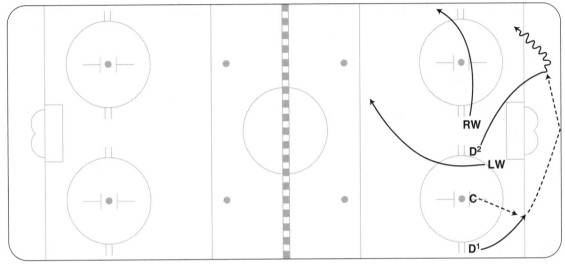

Figure 11.24

■ WIDE RIM

This play can be used to catch the opposition off guard or late in a game when you are up or down by a goal. C wins the draw back to D1, who rims the puck (the Ds may switch sides before the draw to make it an easier rim play). RW goes out to the point and then slants across to support LW (figure 11.25). LW must get to the corner of the blue line before the opposing D. LW has the option to skate with the puck and go through the neutral zone or chip to RW if the opposing defenseman stays in the zone and pinches.

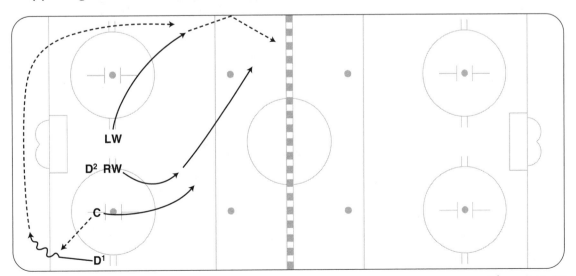

Figure 11.25

■ BREAKAWAY PLAY

C draws the puck back to D1, who quickly skates around the net (figure 11.26). D2 screens to give D1 time to make a play. RW goes hard to the opposing defenseman as if he were going to cover the D. LW slides out to the boards, calling for the pass. RW slants to the center-ice circle. D1 lays or lofts the puck out to RW for a breakaway. RW should have a breakaway because the opposing defense will not have time to react. In leagues that have touch icing, the worst-case scenario is that RW gets the puck in the offensive zone. For automatic icing, the worst-case scenario is that the face-off will come back into your zone

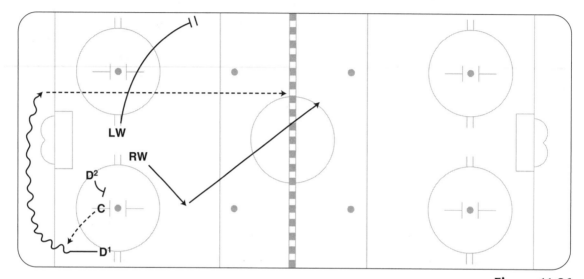

Figure 11.26

■ QUICK-CHANGE PLAY

This is truly a surprise play that should be practiced and used at key moments of the game or season. Once opposing teams know you use it, they may watch for it and therefore be able to react quicker. This play might be used once or twice a year as a trick play when a team is down by a goal with the face-off in their own zone. C draws the puck back to D1 (figure 11.27). RW goes hard to the opposing defenseman as if he were going to cover the D. RW then goes by the D and onto the bench. One forward is waiting at the opposite end of the bench and quickly heads out to the far blue line. LW goes to the boards for a pass. D1 fakes a pass to LW and passes to the new forward at the far blue line.

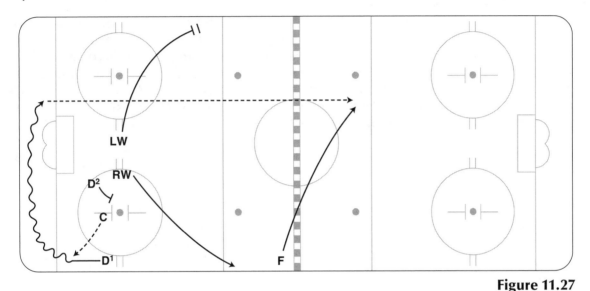

Figure 11.27

Defensive Zone: Lost Draws

There are two variations of alignments that teams may use in their defensive zone. Outlined here are the responsibilities for each player when the face-off is lost. Five Across is the most common alignment, where all players are set to defend; D Back gives you an offensive advantage if you win the draw, but it requires some quick adjustments if you lose.

■ FIVE ACROSS

This common setup is generally used for 80 percent of all defensive zone draws. When C loses the draw, he stays with the other team's center (figure 11.28). RW shoots through on the inside of the circle and pressures the point. LW moves out to the high slot and is ready to go after the other D if a pass is made. D1 and D2 stay with their forwards. The 5 across has become the NHL standard d-zone face off alignment. The only variation is that D2 will be back a few steps with some teams in order to break out quicker when the draw is won. All 5 players have clear assignments and can adjust off of this positioning.

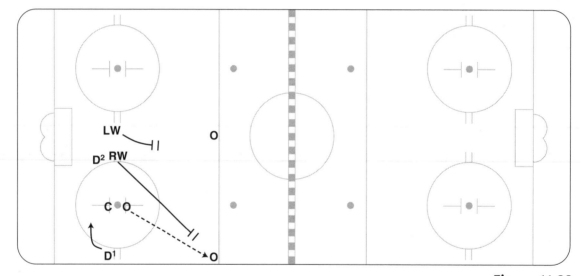

Figure 11.28

■ D BACK

Some teams like to have a D directly behind the center on the draw for an easy breakout (figure 11.29). If you lose the faceoff in this setup, C stays with the other center. RW pressures the boards point, and D1 takes the forward he was lined up against. LW moves into the high slot, ready to pressure the other defenseman if a pass is made. D2 steps up quickly and takes the inside forward.

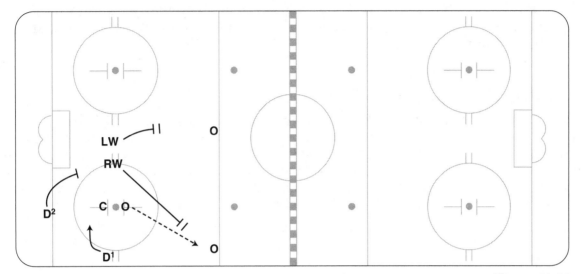

Figure 11.29

Power-Play Face-Offs

It is very important to win or tie up and get possession on power-play draws. If the other team clears the puck, it generally takes the players 20 seconds to get set up again. This is both frustrating and tiring for the power-play unit. Described here are three ways to get possession and set up. Players and coaches should also try to recognize what the penalty-killing unit is trying to do if they win the draw—by doing so you may be able to regain possession even though the draw was lost.

■ TRADITIONAL ALIGNMENT

When C wins or ties up on the draw, both wingers move in to push the puck back to the Ds. On lost draws, RW shoots through to the corner and puts pressure on the opposing D. LW takes away the D-to-D penalty-kill clear or assists RW in the corner. C reacts to apply pressure and support RW and LW (figure 11.30). Although you would like to win all draws because it is so critical to get possession on the power play, you may want to tell the center to tie up his opponent and allow the wingers to help out. The odds of getting possession are better.

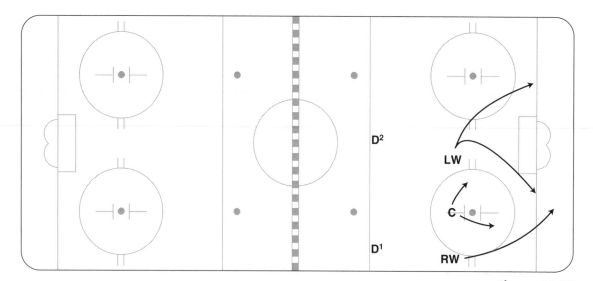

Figure 11.30

■ DOUBLE UP OUTSIDE

In this setup, two forwards are on one side, in order to provide an extra player to try to get puck possession. RW and LW line up along the boards. On a draw where the puck is loose, RW screens and LW pulls the puck back to D1. D2 always lines up in a position that blocks the lane for the opposing center to shoot the puck down the ice immediately off the draw. In this example, if the opposing center was a left shot, then D2 would need to play back a step (figure 11.31). On lost draws, LW shoots through to the corner and ties up the opposing defenseman. RW comes in to get the loose puck.

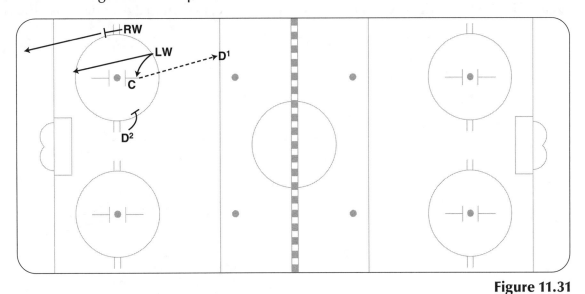

Figure 11.31

■ DOUBLE UP INSIDE

In this setup, two forwards are now on the inside, with D1 on the boards and D2 back on the blue line (figure 11.32). On a draw where the puck is loose, RW and LW move in to get the puck back to D2. RW initially lines up in a position that blocks the lane for the opposing center to shoot the puck down the ice immediately off the draw. In this example, if the opposing center was a left shot, then RW would need to play back a step. On lost draws, RW shoots through to the corner and ties up the opposing defenseman. LW comes in to get the loose puck. There are times off this draw where LW will be open at the net when the puck is loose in the face-off circle. If RW gets the puck when it is loose in the circle, he can make a quick play to LW.

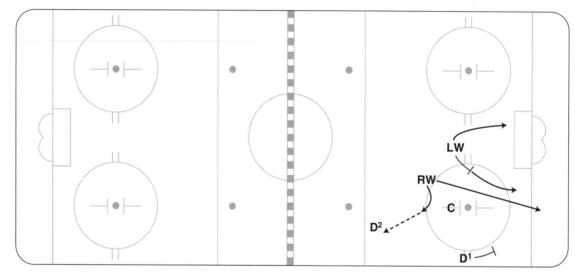

Figure 11.32

Penalty-Kill Face-Offs

Since the face-off is such an important part of the penalty-kill, it was covered in depth in chapter 10 on penalty kills. As mentioned in that chapter, it is very important to gain possession on special teams. Penalty-killing units want to frustrate the power play by making them go back down the ice 200 feet (61 m) to get the puck and start a breakout. More face-off options are presented in chapter 10 (pages 145-148), but here are two common strategies to use after winning draws in the defensive zone.

■ CORNER BUMP

In this situation, when C wins the draw LW drops down to the wide corner (figure 11.33). D1 bumps the puck over to LW, who clears the puck. D2 should screen the opponent's inside winger to provide time for LW to get the puck and shoot it down the ice.

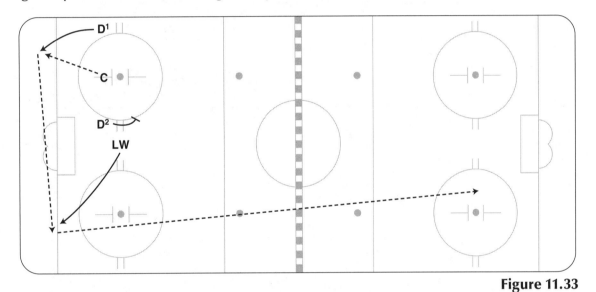

Figure 11.33

■ RIM CLEAR

It is best if the Ds switch sides—this will give the boards-side defenseman the ability to shoot the puck around the boards hard (figure 11.34). C tries to win the draw back to the corner or tie up his opponent and allow the puck to sit in behind. D1 (who is now a left shot) moves in quickly and rims the puck hard on the boards or the glass.

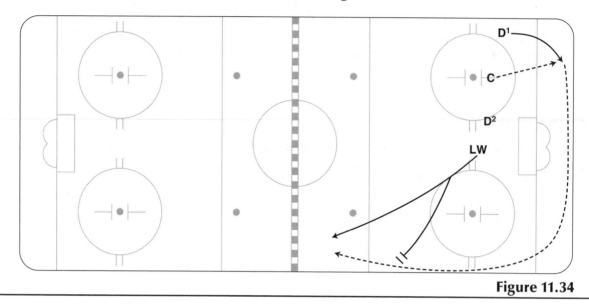

Figure 11.34

Special Face-Off Situations

In this section, we cover face-off strategies for four-on-four play and late-game pulled goaltender situations. Although there aren't as many four-on-four face-offs in a game, it is important that the team be prepared—especially with overtime at most levels using four-on-four play to decide the game. Pulled goaltender situations also don't happen often, but they are very critical for getting that tying goal.

Four-on-Four Face-Offs

We outline one offensive and two defensive alignments for four-on-four situations. On lost draws, coverage is much more difficult when teams are four on four because the center is often tied up taking the face-off and can't get out to the opposing defenseman. Having the D take the draw is a strategy which should be considered.

■ FOUR ACROSS

The center tries to win the draw back to D1 or D2. If the draw is lost F2 must resist the temptation to go out to the boardside defenseman and stay in the slot (figure 11.35). Center battles to get out to pressure the strong side defense. If the puck is passed D-D then F2 moves out in the shooting lane. D1 picks up the opposing center. D2 takes the inside forward. This alignment is the more traditional one used in a teams defensive zone but it does result in problems for the center getting out quickly.

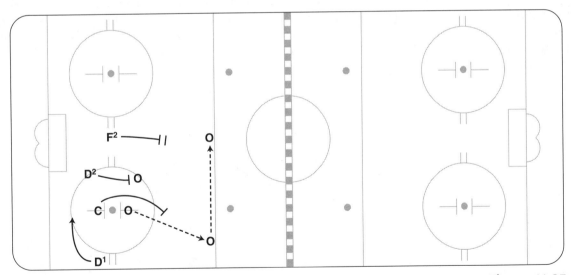

Figure 11.35

■ D TAKES THE DRAW

This sound defensive alignment is not commonly used because it is one where the defense has to practice taking faceoffs. Have D1 take the draw and D2 line up beside the other team's remaining forward (figure 11.36). On a lost draw, D1 and D2 take the other team's forwards, and F1 and F2 go to the opposing defensemen. If the opposition lines up with three up on the draw, then D1 should look at shooting the puck through for F1 and F2 to go two on one.

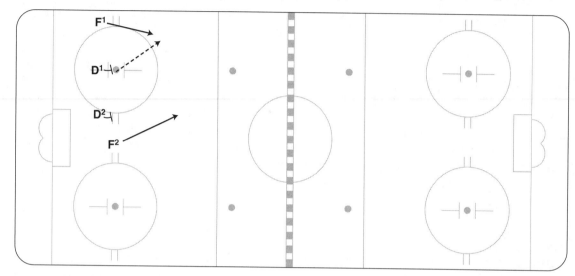

Figure 11.36

■ BOARDS-SIDE ROLL

After winning the face-off in four-on-four situations, teams should make it difficult for the opposition by having a wide option. C takes the draw and wins it back to D1 on the boards (figure 11.37). D1 lines up a few steps back from the hash marks on the boards side. D1 has the option to shoot with F2 at the net or pass to D2 for a one-timer shot. D1 and D2 should switch sides, making it easier for them to shoot.

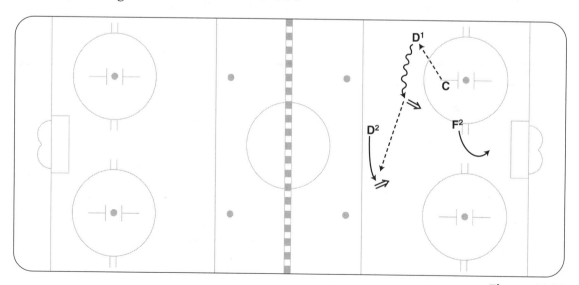

Figure 11.37

Pulled Goaltender

This is an exciting time of the game when a team pulls the goaltender for an extra attacker. Usually it is in the last minute of the game, and the strategy should be to create a chance right off the draw. The play doesn't have to be complicated, but all players need to know what option is being executed. Here are a few strategies.

■ INSIDE-OUT PLAY

C wins the draw or leaves the puck in behind him. LW, C, and EX (extra forward) drive the net (figure 11.38). RW swings to the outside and takes the puck or receives it from D1. C pops out into the slot. RW looks to make a play to C, back to D1, to the front of the net, or to D2 on the back side.

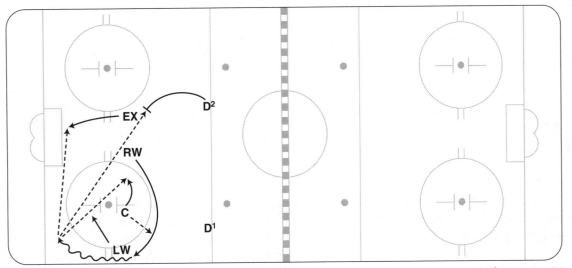

Figure 11.38

■ D SLIDE PLAY

RW is back for the draw, with D2 up on the inside of the circle (figure 11.39). C draws the puck back to D1. RW goes to the net. EX (extra forward) goes to the net. D2 slides out and is ready for a one-timer shot (in this example, D2 is a left shot). D1 may shoot at the net or pass to D2 for a quick shot.

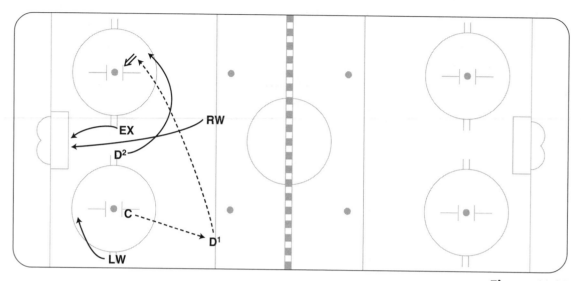

Figure 11.39

■ DOUBLE OPTION

Two forwards line up on the inside (figure 11.40), and one is on the boards (this player must be a left shot). C can draw the puck to the boards so that EX (extra forward) can take a quick shot or the center can tap the puck ahead and make a quick play to the net for LW and RW.

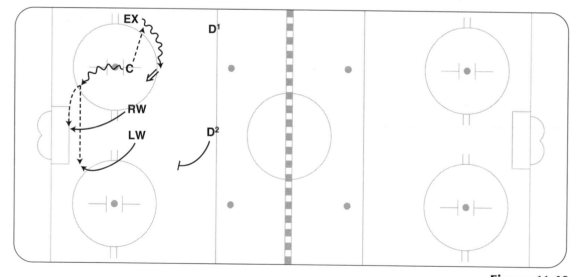

Figure 11.40

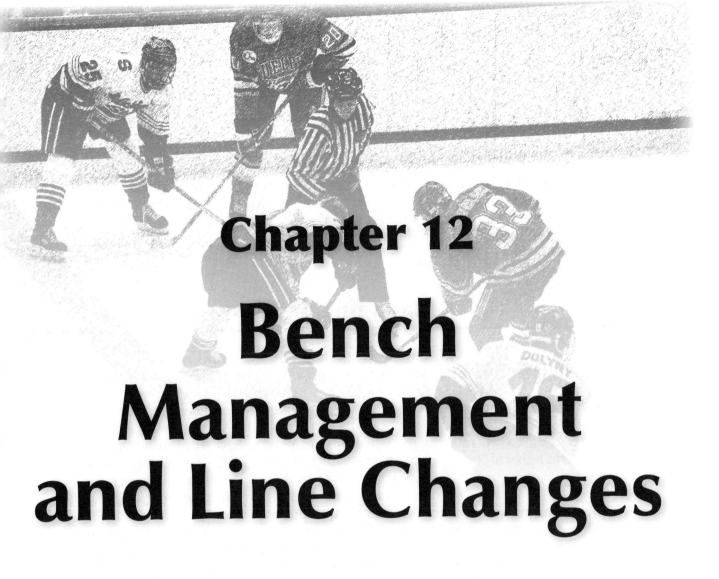

Chapter 12
Bench Management and Line Changes

It has often been said that bench management is the one skill that separates the top coaches from those who are average or below average. Scotty Bowman, recognized as one of the greatest hockey coaches ever, was well respected by opposing players and coaches for his ability behind the bench. What are the inherent skills in a coach who can manage the bench like Scotty Bowman?

The great coaches and players all have in common the ability to "see the ice." They have the unique ability to slow the game down—they see things at a controlled pace and rarely miss anything that happens on the ice. After the game is over (and for some coaches, even years after the game was played), they can recall certain moments clearly. To see the ice with the best, a coach must focus on the game at all times. Don't get distracted by what is happening on the bench or irrelevant things happening on the ice. Stay in emotional control. Stay in the moment. You should always be looking for the one adjustment that will give your team the advantage.

A major aspect of being a great coach is being prepared before the game starts. Know everything you can about the opponent. Who are their top players, who are their weaker players, and what are the tendencies of both? Statistically, is there anything revealing as far as team or individual tendencies? What is their coach like? Does he match lines or shorten his bench? What is his trademark style of play? For example, if you know the opposing coach likes to match lines, then you try to make it hard for him to get the right match. Change on the fly, switch the rotation of your lines (instead of 1-2-3, go 1-2-1-3), or move your top players from line to line. These are all ways to get away from a strong match.

It is important to study the opponent thoroughly; watch them on video if possible, or seek out people who have watched them play. Have a friend or staff member pre-scout them. Ultimately, you want to provide your team with five or six key points based on what you know about the other team. Players will realize that their opportunity for success lies in their ability to execute these points.

Managing Staff

Make sure your staff on the bench know their roles and responsibilities during the game. If you have two assistants on the bench, you should have one coach changing the defense and the other coach providing feedback to the players and to you. Most head coaches run the forward group but there are still a few who like to run the whole bench. Whatever your preference as a coach make sure you instruct your assistants on what you want them to watch for or do. Do you want them to watch for key opposing players, watch for tactical adjustments to make, evaluate your players, or take statistical information? Make sure there is a rink board handy to draw any special plays or for teaching purposes.

Because most games are very hectic and fast paced, it is important to give the players feedback, but it must be concise and specific. The type of feedback players need from assistant coaches should be centered on playing your system or how to react to what the other team is doing. The head coach can provide feedback on effort, work, discipline and game plan details. Assistant coaches can give descriptive feedback to the players during the play, while the head coach should make sure their dialogue is to the point so their focus never strays from the ice surface. It is important to balance constructive with positive feedback, and at all times everyone on the bench should control their emotions. Sometimes coaches would rather wait until after the game to provide feedback, but if the dialogue is short and to the point, you can take advantage of great teaching opportunities on the bench.

Designate which coach will oversee special teams and face-off plays. With most teams special team responsibilities are divided up between both assistants or one assistant and the head coach. It will be important to have one coach in charge of faceoffs and prepared for any special faceoff situations. The most important being pulled goaltender situations. Whether you on the offensive or defensive side in the last minute or two when the goaltender is pulled the team needs to know what to do and who is providing the direction.

In addition, make sure the trainer and equipment manager (if you are fortunate to have both) know their responsibilities. Trainers are mainly there to take care of injuries and make sure the players are hydrated, but they may also keep track of shifts, time the length of shifts, watch for which players are coming out on the other team, and record shots. The equipment person must be available to get sticks when they are broken, sharpen skates, and take care of any equipment problems.

Dealing With Officials

Find out before the game who the officials are and if possible what they are like with regard to calling penalties and receiving feedback. Most refs have a style of calling the game—find out whether they are strict or are inclined to let more go. Once you know this you can prepare the team for what may be called in the game. If you ever challenge a referee, make sure you do it with respect, and above all, know the rules. Over time, coaches who control their emotions, talk to the referees when it is necessary, and cut them some slack on missed calls generally get more of the breaks in the end. Remember, it is a fast-paced game and there is a lot going on between the 10 skaters, so there will be times when the officials miss something or make the wrong call. Far too often now, with the use of video, coaches and managers will look at the game and wonder how the ref made the call that he did—but this is after watching the play several times and maybe in slow motion. Once again, treat officials with respect and you will get respect in return.

Adjusting Your Playing Strategy

First make sure your team is confident in how they have to play to be successful. Your team trademarks should never be altered, but often during the game certain system changes must be made. Again, when to do this and what adjustments to make fall under the category of the art of coaching. The ability to make these decisions comes with experience. If the other team has prepared well and is beating your forecheck with a certain breakout play, then you are going to have to make an adjustment. Often it will be a subtle adjustment; rarely will it be a total switch to another forechecking system. The one area where most adjustments are made is on special teams. Again, because of how prepared opposing teams are, especially in this area, you may be constantly tweaking your power play or penalty kill or making players aware of what their reads should be.

Managing Lines

Before the game, all coaches have to decide whether they are going to match lines and defensive pairs or play whomever they want and let the other team worry about deciding to match. Coaches have different philosophies on matching, with some not wanting to match at all while others want a hard match. The advantages of matching are that you get to put your forwards or defense against players on the other team whom you know they will have success against. For example, it will be difficult for the other team's top offensive players to generate any type of attack if you always have your top defensive players on the ice. Or you may choose to play your top offensive unit head to head against the other team's top unit, thinking that this will challenge your group to play two-way hockey as well as keep them away from the checking unit. Many matching variations can take place in a game, with the most common being matching up your defensemen against the line they will have the most success against. It is much easier to change one or two defensemen during the play to get your match than it is to change a forward line.

The disadvantage of matching is that it disrupts the flow from your bench. Players are constantly changing quickly to maintain the matchups, and there is no rhythm from the bench as when the lines go out 1-2-3. Sometimes it results in a penalty for too many men on the ice because of the constant changing on the fly. With strict matching teams, the checking line will often play a bigger role and be on the ice more than the offensive units. This is another reason why some coaches don't like a hard match.

Make timely decisions about adjusting your lineup. This is the art of coaching, where you trust your instincts and switch line combinations, adjust defensive pairs, or pull the goaltender when you see these players struggling or the team not playing well. Sometimes the best decision is not making a change and letting the players work their way through it. For most coaches, the ability to make the right change comes with experience and also being able to get a read on your players early in the game. You also have to know the personalities of your players. Challenge your athletes, and allow them time to respond before making a change.

Line Changes

Unlike other sports, in the game of hockey, players change on the fly roughly every 40 seconds. It is the coach's job to decide what line is up and the players' job to be ready, but there is a lot more to this coordinated effort.

Hockey games have an ebb and flow woven within their often back and forth movement. One of the undercurrents of any game is developed by the way a team changes its players and shares its ice time. Momentum is the cornerstone of most success, and therefore momentum must be developed and sustained. Much of hockey's momentum comes through effective line changes. Some coaches like to turnover all 4 lines as much as possible and keep tempo from the bench and try to get a contribution from everyone. Others like to flavor their games with much more ice-time for their offensively gifted players and as a result play them a lot more than the other players.

How coaches like to change players and match certain lines is often more of an art than a science. Certain coaches like to match a defensive line against the opponent's offensive line, but the by-product of this course of action is often less ice time for their own offensive players. Some coaches like to turn over all four lines as much as possible, and others like to flavor their games with much more ice time for their offensively gifted players.

Whatever their personal preference, most coaches agree on a number of principles that set at least the ground rules for successful line changes and the momentum they can generate. Let's look at the fundamentals of line changes in the game of hockey.

○ **Make changes while attacking the opponent rather than on the retreat or on the backcheck.** Making sure the puck is either in the offensive zone or moving into the offensive zone ensures there won't be any odd man rushes against you due to a line change. Five players changing on the fly is obviously executed best when the puck is deep in the opponent's zone (figure 12.1). Very seldom does a five-player change happen at one time, and if the whole line is to be changed, often the far-side defenseman will stay on the ice to guard the long three-quarter-ice pass that may spring a breakaway.

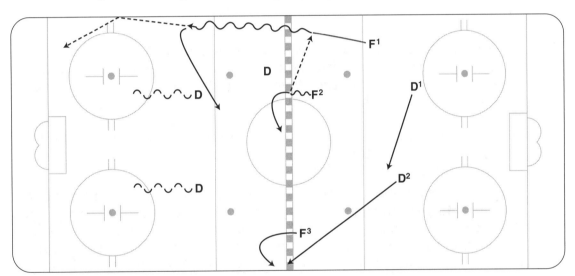

Figure 12.1   Make line changes while attacking the opponent.

○ **Changing on the fly (as the play continues) must happen strategically and geographically.** As a shift nears its end, players closest to the bench will begin the change-on-the-fly process one at a time (figure 12.2). At the younger ages, once one player changes the other players think they also must change, even if they are on the backcheck or pursuing the puck carrier. Logic and strategy play a huge part in when players change. The more dangerous the situation with regard to the opposition generating a scoring chance, the less likely there will be an opportunity to change. For a simple example if players read that there is a high percentage chance that the puck in the neutral zone might get turned over then they should not look to change. Sometimes it means waiting a few more seconds but if the puck does get turned over during a change it will definitely result in a good scoring chance for the other team.

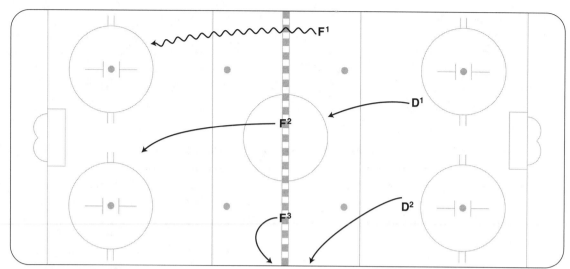

Figure 12.2 As a shift nears its end, players closest to the bench begin the change-on-the-fly process one at a time.

○ **Players on the bench must stay alert at all times.** On-the-fly changes are dynamic and often erratic. Once the coach has signaled which line is up next, it is then up to the players to understand completely whom they are changing with. On many NHL benches, each player calls out the name of the person he is replacing. Encourage your players to communicate ("I've got Johnny" or "Remember Linda is playing center now"). As players rush to make the exchange, have one group go out the gate and another over the boards if possible.

○ **Players on the bench must be aware of on-ice happenings as they are prepping to change.** Often players get so fixated on the person they are going to replace that they do not have a full sense of what is happening on the ice. It is not uncommon for a player to jump on the ice and step right into a puck near the bench before the other player is completely off the ice. Obviously, this results in too many men on the ice and becomes another penalty to kill if caught by an alert official. By being aware of what is happening on the ice, players will be able to react quickly offensively or defensively. Awareness for the player coming on the ice also deals with knowing what your responsibilities are as soon as you get off the bench – are you going on the offense or reacting defensively?

○ **Momentum can be increased by the fluidity of the player changes.** Teams get into a player-changing rhythm, and when all cylinders are firing, this rhythm will create real momentum and be an advantage. Players are allowed 10 feet to make their change at the bench so fluidity refers to executing the change smoothly in this space, at the right time (when players are not too fatigued), and in the right situation. Correct and successful changes save time and energy and when executed perfectly can catch the opponent with tired players on the ice. Can you practice this? Sure you can. Simply set up a drill where players break out and take a shot on goal. Then the line regroups with a second puck, dumps it into the corner, and changes. The new line coming on the ice goes through the same sequence.

O **Timing of changes is critical.** Timing is everything in sport. The timing of how long players stay on the ice and at what point of the shift players change or don't change tells experts a ton about that team's character and identity. Often star players struggling to score goals will cheat in this area. They stay longer than normal and because of this upset the emotional egg carton at times. If the left winger stays on the ice after the center and right winger have changed, this can throw off the synergy of certain line combinations and also anger the next left winger.

For a coach, distributing ice time is much like being the conductor of an orchestra. The goal is to weave each player's talents and strengths into one large sound or force that becomes beautiful and unbeatable.

Bench management has certain constraints and advantages depending on if the game is at home or away. The home-ice coach has last change, and this obviously allows the home coach to better play the chess match that is the game of ice allocation. Away-game coaches look to change their players more often on the fly to get certain desired matchups. NHL coach Mike Keenan suggested the following in our previous book, *Simply the Best*: "That's another thing that I love: the dynamics of the game. People can be asked how many minutes are in a hockey game and the normal answer is 60. Actually there are 720. There are 360 minutes in regulation time distributed between two teams that have 20 players each, so if you give 60 minutes to your goalie (most teams will laugh when I tell them this and say you never do that, because I am always pulling my goaltender) then you've got 300 minutes to distribute on your side with no penalties. The other coach has the same. How you manage this time and who you give it to at what time is an art and you must be able to read the game and your players as it is unfolding."

At every level of play, the entry to the bench and the exit from the bench often tell how cohesive and energetic a team is. You can watch closely at how players change to see what their team spirit is like at certain times of the season. Many people say that the leadership model identifying hockey, even more than in other sports, is that of collaboration. If this is true, then it is most true in the area of bench management and line changes.

Handling the Moment

Finally, if you really want to manage the bench like Scotty Bowman, then you must be able to "handle the moment." Generally, the last 5 minutes in every game are more pressure packed than the first 55, but you have to realize that the key turning point in the game could happen at any time. When the pressure is on—whether the game is tied, you are up or down by one, one team is making a charge and gaining momentum, or the referees have put you down two players—as a coach you need to stay focused on what you are going to control. Never let outside thoughts cloud the picture. Think about what is happening and what needs to be done. Ask for feedback from your assistants. As we mentioned earlier, stay in the moment, and remind your players to do the same. Before the game you should prepare yourself for anything that might happen, so that when it does, it is as if you have been there before . . . and nothing alleviates pressure like being confident in knowing what to do.

Index

Note: The italicized *t* and *f* following page numbers refer to tables and figures, respectively.

About the Authors

Ryan Walter is an assistant coach with the Vancouver Canucks of the National Hockey League. He played more than 1,000 games over 15 seasons with the Washington Capitals, Montreal Canadiens, and Vancouver Canucks. He served as vice president of the National Hockey League Players Association, was honored as the NHL Man of the Year in 1992, and played in the NHL all-star game in 1993. Walter has also served as captain of team Canada in the World Junior tournament and played for team Canada in four World Championships. He has worked as a consultant for several NHL teams and a television analyst for NHL broadcasts. Walter lives in British Columbia, Canada.

Mike Johnston is the head coach and general manager of the Portland Winter Hawks of the Western Hockey League. Previous to this appointment, Johnston spent 9 years as an associate coach in the NHL with Vancouver and Los Angeles. In five of the six seasons he coached with the Vancouver Canucks, they finished with over 90 points, and on two occasions they surpassed the 100-point mark. In 2004 the Canucks won the Northwest Division Championship. Internationally, Johnston has won seven medals while coaching Canada in World Championship events. He won back to back gold medals as an assistant coach with the World Junior Team in 1994 and 1995. At the men's World Championships he has won a gold medal in 1997 and 2007 while capturing a bronze medal in 1995 and a silver medal in 1996 and 2008. Johnston was also on the coaching staff for the Canadian team at the 1998 Olympics in Nagano, Japan. This was the first time in history that NHL players participated in the Olympic games. Johnston holds a master's degree in Coaching Science and presently lives in Portland, Oregon.